Reading Comprehension Acro[ss the Genres]

Grade 8

Contents

Reading Comprehension Across the Genres

A Simple, Flexible Solution for Reading Skills Support

Homework
Assign meaningful, student-centered homework that can be completed in a single sitting.

Practice
Assign independent practice for core reading skills.

Enrichment
Provide students with opportunities for deeper study.

Remediation
Target certain text types or skills that need further attention.

Reinforcement/ Review
Support and review key topics from your curriculum.

Reading Comprehension Across the Genres 8, SV1419023632

Core Reading Skills Instruction

Reading Comprehension Across the Genres provides activity-based instruction for the reading skills that matter most, including . . .

- Identifying main idea and supporting details
- Analyzing author's purpose
- Making inferences
- Drawing conclusions
- Understanding a text's key features
- Making connections to other texts and to the real world
- Extending the text into writing and speaking

Wide Exposure to Genres

Reading Comprehension Across the Genres helps students master core reading skills while providing important exposure to a wide **variety of genres, or text types**, including . . .

- essays
- novels
- letters
- reviews

- cartoons
- poems
- scripts
- journals

- short stories
- advertisements
- functional documents
- tables and charts

Clear, Student-Friendly Lessons

Each lesson in *Reading Comprehension Across the Genres* begins with a **short reading selection** followed by **five exercises**.

Before Reading

Students are introduced to the important aspects of the text, including its type, purpose, structure, and core features.

After Reading

Students complete five exercises that provide careful, student-friendly guidance in understanding the text.

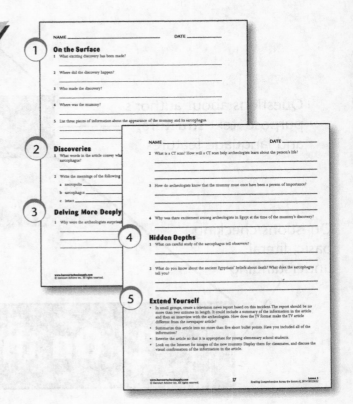

5-Step Exercise Format

The carefully designed exercise format guides students step-by-step through the lessons—taking students from basic understanding to complete comprehension!

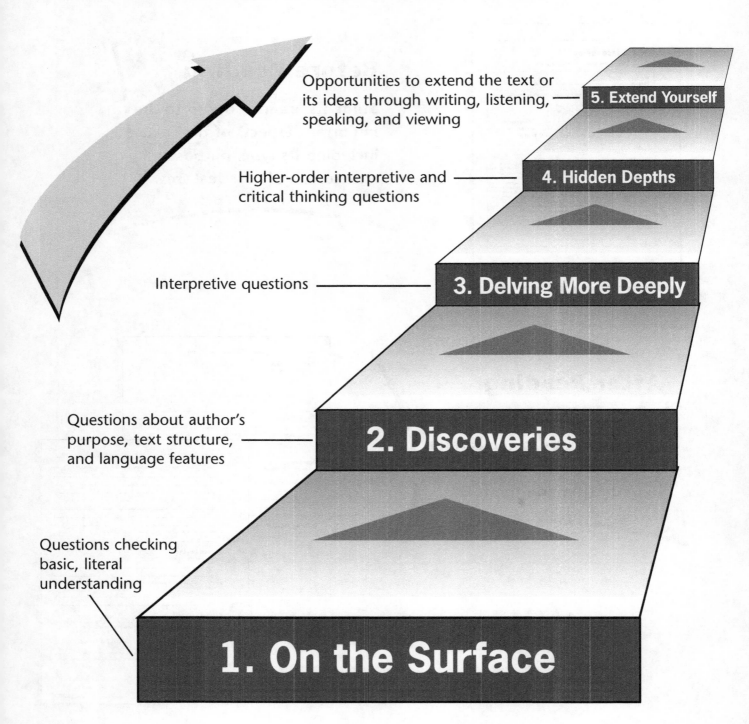

Opportunities to extend the text or its ideas through writing, listening, speaking, and viewing — **5. Extend Yourself**

Higher-order interpretive and critical thinking questions — **4. Hidden Depths**

Interpretive questions — **3. Delving More Deeply**

Questions about author's purpose, text structure, and language features — **2. Discoveries**

Questions checking basic, literal understanding — **1. On the Surface**

Reading Comprehension Across the Genres 8, SV1419023632

Correlation to Genres

Genre or Text Type	Lesson
Informative Nonfiction	8, 14, 17, 24, 31
Narrative Fiction	1, 9, 12, 18
Persuasive/Analytical Documents	11, 15, 16, 19, 20, 22, 28, 30
Functional Documents	5, 7, 10, 21, 25, 26, 29, 32, 34, 35
Formal Letters	4, 33
E-Communications	28
Poetry	13
Scripts/Dramas	6
Journals	2, 3, 27
Cartoons	23

Cross-Curriculum Literacy Links

Curriculum Area	Lesson
Arts	23, 24, 28, 29
Civics and Citizenship	10, 14, 16, 22, 33
Difference and Diversity	9
Gender	19, 27
Geography	6, 13, 15, 22, 23, 30
Health	26, 34, 35
History	1, 6, 8, 11, 12, 13, 14, 17, 18, 19, 30
Mathematics	16, 34
Multicultural Content	15, 34, 35
PE	26
Science	2, 3, 7, 8, 17, 20, 21, 22, 23, 24, 25
Technology	2, 3, 20, 21, 28
Work, Employment, and Enterprise	4, 18, 26, 31

LESSON 1 We're Watching You

Cross-Curriculum Literacy Link: History

Text Type	Narrative
Purpose	To tell a story
Structure	1 Introduction — who or what, where and when
	2 Complication
	3 Series of events
	4 Resolution
Features	Use of past tense; descriptive passages to set the scene and create characters

From **1984**

It was a bright cold day in April, and the clocks were striking thirteen. Winston Smith, his chin nuzzled into his breast in an effort to escape the vile wind, slipped quickly through the glass doors of Victory Mansions, though not quickly enough to prevent a swirl of gritty dust from entering along with him.

The hallway smelt of boiled cabbages and old rag mats. At one end of it a colored poster, too large for indoor display, had been tacked to the wall. It depicted a simply enormous face, more than a meter wide: the face of a man about forty-five, with a heavy black moustache and ruggedly handsome features. Winston made for the stairs. It was no use trying the lift. Even at the best of times it was seldom working, and at present the electric current was cut off during daylight hours. It was part of the economy drive in preparation for Hate Week. The flat was seven flights up, and Winston, who was thirty-nine and had a varicose ulcer above his right ankle, went slowly, resting several times on the way. On each landing, opposite the lift-shaft, the poster with the enormous face gazed from the wall. It was one of those pictures which are so contrived that the eyes follow you about when you move. BIG BROTHER IS WATCHING YOU, the caption beneath it ran.

Inside the flat a fruity voice was reading out a list of figures which had something to do with the production of pig iron. The voice came from an oblong metal plaque like a dulled mirror which formed part of the surface of the right-hand wall. Winston turned a switch and the voice sank somewhat, though the words were still distinguishable. The instrument (the telescreen, it was called) could be dimmed, but there was no way of shutting it off completely. He moved over to the window: a smallish, frail figure, the meagerness of his body merely emphasized by the blue overalls which were the uniform of the Party.

from 1984 by George Orwell. Middlesex: Penguin, 1954. P. 5.

On the Surface

1 What kind of weather is described in the passage?

_____

2 What is the condition of the block of flats that Winston lives in?

_____

3 Why does Winston take the stairs?

_____

4 Why does Winston have to rest?

_____

5 What time is it when Winston gets home, and why is this unusual?

_____

Discoveries

1 These adjectives, and the nouns in parentheses, appear in the excerpt. Circle the ones which have negative connotations (associations).

enormous (face)   vile (wind)   glass (doors)   gritty (dust)   fruity (voice)

2 Circle the correct meanings of the following words, according to their use in the excerpt.

a contrived: accurate; controlled; managed cleverly

b meagreness: generosity; motionlessness; lack of substance

Delving More Deeply

1 What kind of lifestyle do you think Winston has? Give reasons for your answer.

_____

_____

2 Why do you think the telescreen is on continuously and cannot be shut off?

_____

_____

3 Why do you think the caption BIG BROTHER IS WATCHING YOU is in capital letters?

_____

4 Why do you think Winston turns down the volume of his telescreen?

_____

Hidden Depths

1 List the clues which indicate that Winston is living in a restricted society.

_____

_____

2 How would you live your life if you believed you were being monitored? List five things you could not do, especially if the government controlled the monitors.

_____

Extend Yourself

- Write the introduction to a novel about a future where everyone is happy and living conditions are ideal. Your introduction must describe the main character arriving home from work.

- Find a partner and prepare a debate: "Reality TV is a reflection of a sick society."

- What does the character Winston do next? Write half a page.

LESSON 2 Nuclear Fallout

Cross-Curriculum Literacy Links: Science; Technology

Text Type	Diary
Purpose	To reconstruct past experiences by telling events in the order in which they occurred
Structure	1 Introduction — background information about who, where, and when
	2 Series of events in chronological order
	3 A personal comment
Features	Abbreviations, informal language, varied sentences, personal reflections

"A messij 2 the reeda"

Dunno how u found m' dyrees. But sints u hav u mayzwell reed em. Go4it, grok em, I wanna share m' words with sumun. I've printd em neet so u can read em eezy. Nevva bin much with a pen, see. Cum 2 it late, tho Mum guv me n Luce riting lessons when we was littl. Sed evrywun shood know how 2 rite, even if they did hav a VoiceBoy.

So evry day Mum'd rattl out her tin of penz n pensils and mayk us practis. Took away the VoiceBoy and the MetaBook. Turned off the WebWall and hid the Simsuit, and made us jus rite. We luvd it, me n Luce. Doing lettas, bilding words, making thorts take shayp on paper. But then Lucy had her axident and cood only doodl with a grin, and dribbl. Mum stopt the lessons afta that.

So Ive tort m'self, coz words are betta when you mayk em y'self. Warm 'n' alive. I hardly evva yooz the VoiceBoy anymor, or the Metabook. I stopt wen the lectrisity carkt it a cuppla yeers ago. Freekoids trasht the big atomic jenerator near Newcastle. Left a max hole in the ground, and a gray cloud that hung ova the city 4 weeks and gygered evrythin. Even the peepil glowed. That's wen Newcastle became NukeRsol, city of the nukleea sun.

from *CBD* by John Heffernan. NSW: Scholastic, 2000. P. 1.

NAME _____ DATE _____

On the Surface

1 Translate the title of the diary into standard English.

_____

2 Who taught the writer how to write?

_____

3 Why did the writing lessons stop?

_____

4 What happened to the "big atomic jenerator" near Newcastle?

_____

5 What is the new name for Newcastle?

_____

Discoveries

1 Copy two examples of incomplete sentences from the passage. Rewrite them so that they are grammatically correct.

_____

_____

_____

_____

2 Speakers' accents are classified as either broad (a nasal tone), general, or cultivated.

Examine the phonetic spelling of words in the passage and try to guess the writer's speaking style.

For example, if you read out the word "sumun" or "dunno," how does it sound?

How would you classify the writer's speaking style? Circle your answer.

a Broad accent

b General accent

c Cultivated accent

Reading Comprehension Across the Genres 8, SV1419023632

Delving More Deeply

1   What do you think a Voiceboy might be?

_____

2   What do you think has happened to Newcastle? Give reasons for your answer.

_____

_____

3   What is the purpose of the diary?

_____

4   What kind of person is the mother?

_____

5   What age or gender do you imagine the character to be? Why?

_____

Hidden Depths

1   How has technology affected the style and form of language in today's world? Discuss IM, the Internet, and e-mail.

_____

_____

2   What does the language used in the excerpt tell us about the author?

_____

_____

Extend Yourself

•   Collect examples of abbreviations used on IM and e-mail. Rewrite them so they are grammatically correct.

•   Create your own language and write a letter to a friend.

•   Play a game of charades with the class.

LESSON 3 Discoveries

Cross-Curriculum Literacy Link: History; Science

Text Type	Account
Purpose	To reconstruct past experiences by telling events in the order in which they occurred
Structure	**1** Introduction — background information about who, where, and when
	2 Series of events in chronological order
Features	Use of past tense, action verbs; may include adjectives (descriptive language) and quotations

Looking Great After 2,300 Years

The archeologists weren't looking for someone quite so — young. They had traveled from Australia to Egypt to excavate the 4,200-year-old necropolis, or city of the dead, of King Teti. In the winter of 2005, the Egyptian-led team excavated beyond a secret door and found, buried in sand at the bottom of a shaft, a 2,300-year-old mummy.

The mummy is adorned with a mask of gold. Its sarcophagus is covered with brightly painted images of ancient Egyptian gods and goddesses and scenes from the mummification process. The face of the man is painted with colorful details. Zahi Hawass, leading authority on Egyptian antiquities, says that it "may be the most beautiful mummy ever found in Egypt."

Especially amazing: the delicate turquoise beadwork with which ancient Egyptians sometimes adorned coffins is intact. The mummy must have been a person of wealth and importance to have received such an elegant burial.

The mummy was found at the Saqarra Pyramids complex, a hot spot of archeology about fifteen miles south of Cairo, the capital of Egypt. This area is popular with tourists, too, and many visit the Museum of Imenhotep, where this mummy will eventually be displayed, to gaze at the treasures of ancient tombs.

Before the new mummy takes up residence in the museum, however, it will be studied. Archeologists will use CT scanning technology to find out more about who the mummy once was and how he lived and died. This is the same technology that recently was used to examine the mummy of King Tutenkhamen and reveal that he was not murdered, as some had thought, but may have died of infection after breaking a leg.

More exciting finds may be ahead. According to Hawass, an excavation of a "lost" pyramid, now found again, will begin in a few months.

On the Surface

1 What exciting discovery has been made?

_____

2 Where did the discovery happen?

_____

3 Who made the discovery?

_____

4 Where was the mummy?

_____

5 List three pieces of information about the appearance of the mummy and its sarcophagus.

_____

_____

Discoveries

1 What words in the article convey what the excited archeologists saw when they retrieved the sarcophagus?

_____

2 Write the meanings of the following words.

   a necropolis _____

   b sarcophagus _____

   c intact _____

Delving More Deeply

1 Why were the archeologists surprised to find the mummy in this location?

_____

_____

_____

2 What is a CT scan? How will a CT scan help archeologists learn about the person's life?

_____

_____

_____

3 How do archeologists know that the mummy must once have been a person of importance?

_____

_____

_____

4 Why was there excitement among archeologists in Egypt at the time of the mummy's discovery?

_____

_____

Hidden Depths

1 What can careful study of the sarcophagus tell observers?

_____

_____

2 What do you know about the ancient Egyptians' beliefs about death? What does the sarcophagus tell you?

_____

_____

Extend Yourself

- In small groups, create a television news report based on this incident. The report should be no more than two minutes in length. It could include a summary of the information in the article and then an interview with the archeologists. How does the TV format make the TV article different from the newspaper article?

- Summarize this article into no more than five short bullet points. Have you included all of the information?

- Rewrite the article so that it is appropriate for young elementary school students.

- Look on the Internet for images of the new mummy. Display them for classmates, and discuss the visual confirmation of the information in the article.

LESSON 4 Job Hunting

Cross-Curriculum Literacy Links: Work, Employment and Enterprise

Text type	Business letter
Purpose	To apply for a position
Structure	1 Address, date, name (if known), title
	2 Date
	3 Formal greeting
	4 Response to criteria
	5 Sign off
Features	Set layout, formal language

Business Letters

Human Resources Manager
Bing's Department Store
The Mall
Mulberry, MA 01234
3/15/2007

Dear Sir:

I wish to apply for the position of part-time sales assistant in the young men's casual department of Bing's Department Store advertised in the *Mulberry Reminder* on March 12, 2007.

I am a fifteen-year-old high school student in tenth grade at Grovedale High School. I am eager to gain experience in the retail sector. I receive very good grades in English, math, history, and Spanish.

My interests include sports and reading. I am the captain of the Grovedale basketball team as well as being a good soccer goalie. These sports have allowed me to develop my skills as a team player. I am a reliable and punctual person, and I would enjoy the opportunity to learn about the workforce.

Please find enclosed my résumé and a reference. I am available for an interview at your convenience.

Sincerely,

Jasper Clark

Jasper Clark

On the Surface

1   How old is the applicant?

_____

2   What job is he applying for?

_____

3   What is a reference?

_____

4   Why does the applicant mention that he is reliable and punctual?

_____

Discoveries

1   Simple sentences are sentences that contain one main idea. Circle the simple sentences below.

   a   My interests include sports and reading.

   b   I am a reliable and punctual person, and I would enjoy the opportunity to learn about the workforce.

   c   I am a fifteen-year-old high-school student in tenth grade at Grovedale High School.

   d   I receive very good grades in English, math, history, and Spanish.

2   Business letters have a formal tone. Just as we give spoken language a tone, we can give writing a tone by selecting particular words and sentence structures.

   How is a formal tone created in the letter?

_____

_____

_____

Delving More Deeply

1 What kind of person is the applicant?

_____

2 What is a résumé, and how does it differ from a letter of application?

_____

_____

_____

3 What aspects of Jasper's academic work would be most relevant to the position?

_____

4 Do you think the applicant's interest in sports is relevant to the job?

_____

Hidden Depths

1 What research would you recommend the applicant complete before attending a job interview?

_____

_____

2 This job was advertised in the newspaper. List at least two other ways of finding out about jobs.

_____

_____

3 What are the benefits of teenagers having part-time jobs?

_____

Extend Yourself

• Research how to write a résumé, and put together one for yourself. Make this a résumé for your own search for a part-time job.

• Find two job advertisements from different fields. Write a letter in response to each of these advertisements, taking care to adjust your style according to the job.

• Write an advertisement for your "dream" job.

• Write a list of guidelines advising students on how to find part-time work.

LESSON 5 "Metabolism" to "Metatarsus"

Text Type	Dictionary
Purpose	To give the meaning, pronunciation, grammatical use, and history of words in a language

Structure
1 Headword
2 Syllabification and Pronunciation
3 Part of speech
4 Definitions
5 Phrases and compounds
6 Derivatives
7 Cross-references
8 Etymology

Features Abbreviations, font changes

---

metabolize

metabolism me·tab·o·lism / m-tb-lzm / n. **1.** The chemical processes occurring within a living cell or organism that are necessary for the maintenance of life. In metabolism some substances are broken down to yield energy for vital processes while other substances, necessary for life, are synthesized. **2.** The processing of a specific substance within the living body: *water metabolism; iodine metabolism.* From Greek *metabol*, change, from *metaballein*, to change : *meta-*, meta- + *ballein*, to throw.

metabolize me·tab·o·lize / m-tb-lz / v. **(-zing)** v. *trans.* **1.** To subject (a substance) to metabolism. **2.** To produce (a substance) by metabolism. v. *intrans.* To undergo change by metabolism.

metacarpus met·a·car·pus / mt-kärps / Inflected forms: pl. **met·a·car·pi** (-p) **1.** The part of the human hand that includes the five bones between the fingers and the wrist. **2.** The corresponding part of the forefoot of a quadruped.

metal met·al / mtl / — **1.** *abbr.* **M** Any of a category of electropositive elements that usually have a shiny surface, are generally good conductors of heat and electricity, and can be melted or fused, hammered into thin sheets, or drawn into wires. Typical metals form salts with nonmetals, basic oxides with oxygen, and alloys with one another. **2.** An alloy of two or more metallic elements. **3.** An object made of metal. **4.** Basic character; mettle. **5.** Broken stones used for road surfaces or railroad beds. **6.** Molten glass, especially when used in glassmaking. **7.** Molten cast iron. **8.** Printing Type made of metal. **9.** Music Heavy metal.
...

metallic me·tal·lic / m-tlk / adj. **1.** Of, relating to, or having the characteristics of a metal. **2.** Containing a metal: *a metallic compound.* **3.** Having a quality suggesting or associated with metal,

metatarsus

especially: **a.** Lustrous; sparkling: *metallic colors.* **b.** Sharp-tasting: *an unpleasant, metallic flavor.* **me·talli·cal·ly** — ADVERB
...

metallurgy met·al·lur·gy / mtl-ûrj / **1.** The science that deals with procedures used in extracting metals from their ores, purifying and alloying metals, and creating useful objects from metals. **2.** The study of metals and their properties in bulk and at the atomic level. New Latin *metallrgia*, from Greek *metallourgos*, miner, worker in metals : *metallon*, a mine, metal + *-ourgos*, -worker (from *ergon*, work)

metamorphic met·a·mor·phic / mt-môrfk / **1.** Of, relating to, or characterized by metamorphosis. **2.** *Geology* Changed in structure or composition as a result of metamorphism. Used of rock.

metamorphose met·a·mor·phose / mt-môrfz, -fs / v. **(-sing) 1.** To change into a wholly different form or appearance; transform. **2.** To subject to metamorphosis or metamorphism.

metamorphosis met·a·mor·pho·sis / mt-môrf-ss / Inflected forms: pl. **met·a·mor·pho·ses** (-sz) **1.** A transformation, as by magic or sorcery. **2.** A marked change in appearance, character, condition, or function. **3.** *Biology* A change in the form and often habits of an animal during normal development after the embryonic stage. Metamorphosis includes, in insects, the transformation of a maggot into an adult fly and a caterpillar into a butterfly and, in amphibians, the changing of a tadpole into a frog. Latin *metamorphsis*, from Greek, from *metamorphoun*, to transform : *meta-*, meta- + *morph*, form.

metaphor met·a·phor / mt-fôr, -fr / **1.** A figure of speech in which a word or phrase that ordinarily designates one thing is used to designate another, thus making an implicit comparison, as in *"a sea of troubles"* or *"All the world's a stage"*

(Shakespeare). **2.** One thing conceived as representing another; a symbol: "*Hollywood has always been an irresistible, prefabricated metaphor for the crass, the materialistic, the shallow, and the craven*" (Neal Gabler, *New York Times Book Review* November 23, 1986). Middle English *methaphor*, from Old French *metaphore*, from Latin *metaphora*, from Greek, transference, metaphor, from *metapherein*, to transfer : *meta-*, meta- + *pherein*, to carry; see **bher-**[1] in Appendix I.

metaphysical met·a·phys·i·cal / mt-fz-kl / **1.** Of or relating to metaphysics. **2.** Based on speculative or abstract reasoning. **3.** Highly abstract or theoretical; abstruse. **4a.** Immaterial; incorporeal. See synonyms at **immaterial**. **b.** Supernatural.

5. often **Metaphysical** Of or relating to the poetry of a group of 17th-century English poets whose verse is characterized by an intellectually challenging style and extended metaphors comparing very dissimilar things. ...

metatarsus met·a·tar·sus / mt-tärss/ n. Inflected forms: pl. **met·a·tar·si** (-s, -s) **1.** The middle part of the human foot that forms the instep and includes the five bones between the toes and the ankle. **2.** The corresponding part of the hind foot in quadrupeds or of the foot in birds.

From The American Heritage Dictionary of the English Language: Fourth Edition. 2000.

On the Surface

1 What is the noun form of *metabolize*?

_____

2 What is the adjectival form of *metal*?

_____

3 Explain in your own words the meaning of *metallurgy*.

_____

4 Give an example of a metaphor.

_____

_____

Discoveries

1 What is the difference between a simile and a metaphor?

_____

_____

2 Translate the following similes into metaphors.

a The sun is like a gold coin.

_____

b The sky is like a blue blanket.

_____

_____

Delving More Deeply

1   What might be the concerns of metaphysical poets?

   a Creating poetry about metal objects

   b Creating poetry which is about physical existence only

   c Creating poetry that reflects philosophically on life and death

2   The prefix *meta-* means "change" or "occurring behind or after." How does knowing this help you define the word *metamorphosis?*

   _____

3   Make up your own way to write the pronunciation for the word *phone.*

   _____

4   What kind of information is provided in an etymology?

   _____

Hidden Depths

1   In pairs, write a short story called "Metamorphosis."

2   Write some of your own similes and metaphors for the sun, the sea, and the sky.

   _____

   _____

   _____

Extend Yourself

• Read a poem by metaphysical poet John Donne, and write your interpretation of it in 500 words.

• Read the story "Metamorphosis" by Franz Kafka. In your own words, summarize what happens.

• Write a poem that uses an extended metaphor.

LESSON 6 Star Cross'd Lovers

Cross-Curriculum Literacy Links: History; Geography

Text Type	Script
Purpose	To entertain
Structure	1 Introduction — who or what, where and when
	2 Complication
	3 Series of events
	4 Resolution
Features	Direct speech, stage directions

From Romeo and Juliet

The prologue

[Enter CHORUS]

Two households, both alike in dignity,

In fair Verona, where we lay our scene,

From ancient grudge break to new mutiny,

Where civil blood makes civil hands unclean.

From forth the fatal loins of these two foes

A pair of star-cross'd lovers take their life;

Whose misadventur'd piteous overthrows

Doth with their death bury their parents' strife.

The fearful passage of their death-mark'd love,

And the continuance of their parents' rage,

Which, but their children's end, nought could remove,

Is now the two hours' traffic of our stage;

The which if you with patient ears attend,

What here shall miss, our toil shall strive to mend.

[Exit.]

from *Romeo and Juliet* by William Shakespeare. I. i. 1–14

On the Surface

1   Where is the play set?

   _____

2   What happens to the lovers?

   _____

3   What is a prologue?

   _____

4   What happens to the feud after the lovers die?

   _____

5   What is a modern word for *foe?*

   _____

Discoveries

1   An iamb is a metrical foot and is an unstressed syllable followed by a stressed syllable. Iambic pentameter is a five-foot line. That is, it consists of ten syllables and every second syllable is stressed.

   Count the syllables in each line of the prologue. Are there ten? _____

   Is every second syllable stressed? _____

2   Underline the stressed syllables in the following lines.

   a   Two households both alike in dignity

   b   In fair Verona where we lay our scene

   c   From ancient grudge break to new mutiny

Delving More Deeply

1   What is meant by "star-cross'd lovers"?

   a   Fate destroys their chances of happiness.

   b   The lovers are born under opposite star signs.

2   What might be meant by two families "both alike in dignity"?

   a   They have the same social status and importance.

   b   Both families behave in a dignified way.

3 What is meant by "death-mark'd love"?

_____

_____

4 Copy out the lines from the passage which mean a new fight has occurred and people have been killed.

_____

_____

_____

Hidden Depths

1 What is the purpose of telling the play's outcome at the beginning?

_____

_____

_____

2 What do families argue about?

_____

Extend Yourself

- Write a love story that would be of interest to your age group. Aim to create an obstacle that the couple must overcome before they can begin dating.

- Research the history of Valentine's Day. Create a list of the most overblown declarations of love.

- View a film version of *Romeo and Juliet*. Create a poster advertising it.

 **LESSON 7 Science Experiment**

Cross-Curriculum Literacy Link: Science

Text Type	Procedure
Purpose	To give instructions or show how something is accomplished through a series of steps
Structure	1 Opening statement of goal or aim
	2 Materials required listed in order of use
	3 Series of steps listed in chronological order
Features	Logical series of steps, may use technical language and diagrams

Chemical Activity in Metals

What is the order of chemical activity of some metals?

Equipment:

9 test tubes

cold water

small pieces of the following metals: copper, magnesium, iron, zinc, calcium

acid

Procedure 1:

Clean the metals. Fill each test tube with 2 cm of water.

Place each metal in a separate test tube.

Record the rate at which the bubbles form: fast, medium, slow, or none.

Which metals did not make the water bubble?

Place those that did make the water bubble in order of fastest to slowest.

Procedure 2:

Clean the metals but not the calcium. Do not use the calcium in this part of the experiment.

Using four new test tubes, place each metal in 2 cm of acid.

Which metals cause bubbles to form in acid?

Place those that caused the acid to bubble in order of record, showing which metals make the acid bubble, in order of fastest to slowest.

Which metal is most reactive?

On the Surface

1   What is the purpose of this experiment?

_____

2   How should the metals be prepared?

_____

3   How much water should be placed in each of the test tubes?

_____

4   List the metals to be tested in both experiments.

_____

5   What is the difference between Procedure 1 and Procedure 2?

_____

_____

Discoveries

1   The meaning of *dilute* is "to lower the concentration of a substance, especially by adding water; to weaken."

Write a sentence using the word *dilute*.

_____

_____

2   Imperative verbs command you to perform an action (for example, "Close that door!") Instructions rely on such verbs to make the procedure clear. Copy out two imperative verbs from the procedures.

_____

Delving More Deeply

1   Which branch of science would this experiment come from?

_____

2   Make a list of everything you would need to perform the experiments.

_____

3   What conclusion might you draw from this experiment?

_____

4   Why is chemistry an important subject?

_____

5   Would diagrams make these procedures clearer?

_____

_____

Hidden Depths

1   Why do you think science is a required subject in most public schools? Do you agree with this policy?

_____

_____

_____

2   How important is the connection between ethics and science? Consider recent TV commercials that advertise pharmaceutical products directly to the general public.

_____

_____

Extend Yourself

- Find out about careers in chemistry. Report your findings to your class.
- Make a poster encouraging students to study science.
- Invite a chemist or other scientist to give a lecture and demonstration at your school.
- Create a web page about an important scientist such as Albert Einstein or Isaac Newton.

LESSON 8 *All That Glitters . . .*

Cross-Curriculum Literacy Links: Science; History

Text Type	Explanation
Purpose	To explain how or why things are as they are or how things work
Structure	1 A general statement
	2 Series of events in chronological or logical order
	3 Concluding statement
Features	Logical sequence of details or ideas; may use headings, diagrams and tables

Metals

Gold, silver, copper, lead, iron, tin, and mercury are the metals that were known in ancient times. One of the main reasons they were found first is that many of them exist as pure metals. For example, gold is often found pure and does not have to be separated from a compound. Other metals such as copper exist mainly as a compound called an ore.

The reason most metals are not found as pure metals is that they are chemically too reactive. Sodium is the most reactive element, and it was not discovered until 1807. This is because its high chemical reactivity makes it very hard to extract from its compounds.

Metal is found in rocks called ores. The separation of a metal from its ore depends on the level of chemical activity. There are two main methods:

1   the less active metals are extracted in a blast furnace, for example, iron, lead;

2   the more active metals are extracted using electricity, for example, aluminum, sodium.

Activity	Metal
Most active	sodium
	calcium
	magnesium
	aluminum
	zinc
	chromium
	iron
	nickel
	tin
	lead
	copper
	mercury
	silver
	platinum
Least active	gold

On the Surface

1   List the elements known to ancient peoples.

_____

2   Explain why these metals were found first.

_____

_____

3   Give an example of a metal that exists mainly as a compound.

_____

4   What is the most reactive element listed?

_____

5   Why wasn't sodium discovered until 1807?

_____

_____

Discoveries

1   Write the meanings of the following words as they are used in the text. Use a dictionary if you
    are unsure of a word's meaning.

   a   elements

   _____

   _____

   b   ore

   _____

   c   compound

   _____

2   A simple sentence has one clause, for example: The day is hot. A compound sentence has two
    main clauses linked by a conjunction, for example: The day is hot and the sky is blue.

    Go through the passage on "Metals" and copy a compound sentence.

   _____

   _____

Delving More Deeply

1   How are the more active metals extracted?

_____

2   What branch of science does this article pertain to?

_____

3   Are any aspects of the instructions unclear? How else might the chart be organized to present the information clearly?

_____

_____

Hidden Depths

1   Why do you think metals such as gold have been described as pure?

_____

2   Describe the language and sentence structures used here. Why has this style of writing been used?

_____

Extend Yourself

• Create a mnemonic in order to memorize the table.

• Create a simple diagram as an alternative to the table.

• Create a map showing where precious metals come from in the world. Which patterns, in terms of wealth in those countries, can you see?

LESSON 9 A Long Way from Home

Cross-Curriculum Literacy Link: Difference and Diversity

Text Type Narrative, science fiction
Purpose To tell a story
Structure 1 Introduction — who or what, where and when
2 Complication
3 Series of events
4 Resolution
Features Use of past tense, pronouns, technical or scientific language

Ray Bradbury is a writer who is famous for his science fiction stories. This genre often explores the question, "What would happen if . . . ?"

From "The Meteor"

It was a long way back to the hills. The sun was low in the sky by the time he reached the spot where the collapsed gallery gave on to the hillside. Passing the pile of earth, from which he had emerged earlier that day like a crushed and frightened rabbit, his foot struck something metallic. The flashlight! He pocketed it thankfully.

Higher. Here was the real entrance to the mine. He went into the blackness, holding the beam in front of him, trying not to think of the nightmare thing he had seen there, trying not to open his mind to the voices he expected to sound within it at any moment. His brain cringed!

But nothing happened; and the passage seemed to be widening.

Suddenly it was an almost circular chamber hewn out of rock; and at the same time he heard the sounds of work around the buried spaceship-the tapping and scraping, like the activities of underground dwarfs in fairy tales.

And then he heard a sound like an intake of breath. He swung the torch.

"Who's there?"

His beam flashed across the space.

"Ellen!"

She stood there, ten yards from him, unhurt, cool.

"Ellen! Are you all right? I . . ."

Then she spoke. Or didn't speak. The voice was not a sound — not words — but a set of questionings popping thought-like into his head:

"Why have you come back? Who have you brought with you? Why do you wish to destroy us?"

He felt weak. He had lost her. This was not Ellen; or if it was Ellen's body in front of him, something else was in possession.

He said: "I came back to warn you. Some men of my world are on their way here . . ."

"I know" — her thought-voice said inside him — "there are a dozen cars on the road from the town this minute."

"I tried to stop them . . ."

"We are not yet ready. Not quite ready."

"Take me to . . . to your friends. I want to help."

"Come."

He followed her; and soon the ground sloped, the walls widened and the work-sounds became a roar. There was light, blue and vibrant — the naked light of energy — and a prickling went over him as he breathed an air like the aftermath of storm, all washed clean with electricity.

For the second time in his life he saw the spaceship, the six-sided glove with its hull aglow, as if the contained force of its motors was a sort of lifeblood making its plates flush like flesh.

Around the ship the rock and earth had been cleared; above it the massed debris shut out the sun. Busy round the open port, through which strange mechanisms could be glimpsed, were a dozen figures familiar as home. He recognized the backs of Doctor Snell, of Frank . . . and then one of the figures turned and came towards him. He nearly collapsed . . .

He stared open-jawed at *himself*!

from "The Meteor" by Ray Bradbury, in *Classic Science Fiction*, Ed. Peter Haining. London: Pan, 1998. p. 44.

On the Surface

1   At what time of day does the main character reach the spaceship?

_____

2   Describe the mood or feelings of the narrator. Find words in the text to support your opinion.

_____

_____

_____

3   Why is he relieved to find the flashlight?

_____

4   How does Ellen communicate with the narrator?

_____

5   Why is the narrator so surprised at the end of the passage?

_____

Discoveries

1   Underline the correct definitions for the words as they appear in the text.

   a   cringe: to shrink in fear; to cry; to shout

   b   aftermath: after a math lesson; results of an event; rain

   c   debris: fragments; a tunnel; a blockage

2 Writers use similes to make their work more vivid. Explain the meaning conveyed by the following similes.

a "like a crushed and frightened rabbit"

_____

b "like the activities of underground dwarfs in fairy tales"

_____

Delving More Deeply

Answer true or false.

1 Some men of the narrator's world are on their way to the spaceship. _____

2 The narrator does not wish to help them get away. _____

3 The narrator meets his friend Ellen, who he knows very well. _____

4 There are replicas of people on the spaceship. _____

5 Ellen is possessed by another controlling intelligence. _____

Hidden Depths

1 Do you believe there is another intelligent life form in the universe? Explain why or why not.

_____

_____

2 Find out about cloning. List the arguments for and against cloning. Hold a class debate.

_____

_____

Extend Yourself

- Write an imaginative story to warn about the dangers of cloning.
- Read a collection of Ray Bradbury's stories. Write a review of one of them.
- Watch the 1953 sci-fi movie *It Came from Outer Space*, based on Bradbury's short story. Write a review of the movie, or design a movie poster.

NAME _____ DATE _____

 # A Politician Speaks

Cross-Curriculum Literacy Link: Civics and Citizenship

Text Type	Exposition
Purpose	To put forward an argument or particular point of view
Structure	Justifications of position in a logical order
Features	Persuasive language

An Open Letter to Our Citizens

I've had the pleasure and the privilege of serving you, my fellow citizens of Marshtown, in the office of mayor for three years now. Today I am announcing my intention to run for reelection, for another term of service to my city and my neighbors. I would like to take this opportunity to remind my readers of the work our council has done for you in the last three years. I also want to talk about the work I hope to do in my second term.

These three years have been a period of great growth for our city. Our population has grown by 10% as new families and new businesses have chosen to make Marshville their home. The council and I have been busy with zoning decisions that will keep our neighborhoods free of busy traffic while making sure that everyone can get to the stores.

Growth brings challenges, of course. During my tenure as mayor, we have passed a bond election to build two new elementary schools. One is serving students already, and the other will open in the fall. We are also working on plans for another middle school and a new athletic complex that will serve the schools and the community. It has been an honor to work with the many committees that plan these great changes.

Growth also brings a few headaches, especially in the traffic area. I have worked with state and federal offices to bring in money for upgrading existing roads and building new ones. The ground has been broken for a loop around the city that will make it easier to get to where you want to go — or to avoid the traffic and go around.

We've accomplished so much. In my next term, I want to see these projects through to completion. And I want to start one other project that I believe is critical to our city's health and happiness: We need to protect the greenbelt that runs along our river. We need to clear brush and debris, build parks and playgrounds, and create a trail system for people to walk and jog on. Great cities have green areas where people can play, exercise, or just take it easy.

I hope I will have your support as I run for a second term. Thank you for taking the time to read this letter. Let's work together to make Marshtown marvelous!

On the Surface

1 What kind of document is the passage, and what is its purpose?

_____

2 Who has written the letter, and who are its recepients?

_____

3 What changes has Marshtown seen in the last three years?

_____

_____

4 What must Marshtown build to keep up with the growth?

_____

Discoveries

1 Write the meanings of the following words.

a privilege _____

b tenure _____

c upgrading _____

d greenbelt _____

2 What literary sound effect does the last line use, and why?

_____

Delving More Deeply

1 Why does the writer use the pronouns *we* and *our* so often in the letter?

_____

_____

2 What is a traffic loop?

_____

_____

_____

Reading Comprehension Across the Genres 8, SV1419023632

3 Is the writer an experienced politician? How can you tell?

_____

_____

4 Why does the writer think a greenbelt for the city should be a priority?

_____

_____

Hidden Depths

1 What are zoning issues and why do they matter?

_____

_____

_____

2 Would you vote for the writer, based on the letter? Explain.

_____

_____

Extend Yourself

- Locate other examples of persuasive writing and/or propaganda, such as advertisements on television or the Internet, film reviews, leaflets, and flyers. Compare and contrast the language used and issues raised.

- Write a sixty-second radio ad for the mayor. Practice it, time it, and read it to your classmates. What are the challenges of such short ads?

 **LESSON 11** # A Modern Classic

Cross-Curriculum Literacy Link: History

Text Type Book review
Purpose To provide an opinion on a book
Structure **1** Context — background information on the text
2 Description of the text (including characters and plot)
3 Concluding statement (judgment, opinion, or recommendation)
Features Formal language, use of quotations and examples from the book

Book Review: To Kill a Mockingbird

"It's when you know you're licked before you begin, but you begin anyway and you see it through no matter what." These are the stirring words of lawyer Atticus Finch as he prepares to defend a wrongly accused man. *To Kill a Mockingbird* is a classic studied in schools all over the world. Published in 1960, this novel has never been out of print. The author, Harper Lee, has written only one novel, and much of the book is based on her own experiences. The story is told through the eyes of Scout Finch, the young tomboy daughter of lawyer Atticus Finch. Set in the deep American south of the 1930s in a small town called Maycomb, the novel has much to say about racial prejudice. However, it is also a book about the trials of growing up. Scout and her brother Jem have to deal with gossiping neighbours and vicious rumors. The focus of their childhood world is the mysterious Boo Radley, who has lived as a recluse for twenty years. Faced with a lack of information, the children imagine him to be a monster, "a malevolent phantom" who would be ready to murder them at any moment. It takes a number of painful experiences for them both to realize the false nature of their assumptions. In the second half of the novel, the action shifts to the trial of Tom Robinson, an African American man accused of assaulting a white woman.

Atticus knows he cannot win, but he fights heroically for justice in a biased trial and gives one of the most moving speeches in literature. Lee's strengths are her characterization and her powers of description. Maycomb is described as a tired old town where "ladies end their days dusted with talcum." It is hard to read the novel without being inspired by the model of good citizenship provided by Atticus Finch. This is a book that reminds us to be idealistic. It will appeal to readers who love history, a good story, and a writer who delivers a worthwhile message.

On the Surface

1 Where and when is the novel set?

_____

2 What is the occupation of the father?

_____

3 Why are there rumors about Boo Radley?

_____

4 What are the themes or important topics of the novel?

_____

5 Why is Atticus Finch such an inspiring character?

_____

Discoveries

1 Underline the correct definitions of the words as they appear in the text.

   a biased: preferring one side; bypassing; being fair

   b malevolent: violent; ghostly; evil

   c idealistic: naïve; thoughtful; focusing on the positive aspects of a situation

2 What is the difference between plot and theme? Give an example from texts you have studied this year.

_____

_____

Delving More Deeply

1 Why do you think the reviewer refers to the novel as a classic? What in your opinion is a "classic," be it in film or fiction? Give some examples.

_____

_____

2 Does this review make you want to read the novel? Give reasons for your answer.

_____

_____

3 What is idealism? Are students encouraged to be idealistic? Is this a positive quality?

_____

_____

4 How many novels do you read that have positive messages? Give some examples.

_____

_____

Hidden Depths

1 Why has the reviewer used direct quotations from the book?

_____

_____

2 List two novels that you would consider to be classic American novels.

_____

_____

Extend Yourself

- Watch the film of the novel and write a comparison.
- Write a 250-word negative review of a book and give reasons for your response. Be fair!
- Write a short story from an outsider's point of view.

LESSON 12 Pioneer Days

Cross-Curriculum Literacy Links: History

Text Type	Description
Purpose	To describe the characteristic features of a particular person or thing
Structure	1 Opening statement — introduction to the subject
	2 Characteristic features of the subject
	3 Concluding statement (optional)
Features	Details that allow the reader to imagine and understand the subject

from *Letters of a Woman Homesteader* (Wyoming, 1909)

I have heard of clean people, but Gavotte is the cleanest man I ever saw. The cabin floor was so white I hated to step upon it. The windows shone, and at each there was a calico curtain, blue-and-white check, unironed but newly washed. In one window was an old brown pitcher, cracked and nicked, filled with thistles. I never thought them pretty before, but the pearly pink and the silvery green were so pretty and looked so clean that they had a new beauty. Above the fireplace was a great black eagle which Gavotte had killed, the wings outspread and a bunch of arrows in the claws. In one corner near the fire was a washstand, and behind it hung the fishing-tackle. Above one door was a gun-rack, on which lay the rifle and shotgun, and over the other door was a pair of deer-antlers. In the center of the room stood the square home-made table, every inch scrubbed. In the side room, which is the bedroom, was a wide bunk made of pine plank that had also been scrubbed, then filled with fresh, sweet pine boughs, and over them was spread a piece of canvas that had once been a wagon sheet, but Gavotte had washed it and boiled and pounded it until is was clean and sweet. That served for a sheet.

. . .

Gavotte did himself proud getting supper. We had trout and the most delicious biscuit. Each of us had a crisp, tender head of lettuce with a spoonful of potato salad in the center. We had preserves made from canned peaches and the firmest yellow butter. Soon it was quite dark and we had a tiny brass lamp which gave but a feeble light, but it was quite cool so we had a blazing fire which made it light enough.

When supper was over, Zebbie called us out and asked us if we could hear anything. We could hear the most peculiar, long-drawn, sighing wail that steadily grew louder and nearer. I was really frightened, but he said it was the forerunner of the windstorm that would soon strike us. He said it was wind coming down Crag Cañon, and in just a few minutes it struck us like a cold wave and rushed, sighing, on down the cañon. We could hear it after it had passed us, and it was perfectly still around the cabin. Soon we heard the deep roar of the coming storm, and Zebbie called the hounds in and secured the door. The sparks began to fly up the chimney. Jerrine lay on a bearskin before the fire, and Mrs. O'Shaughnessy and I sat on the old blue "settle" at one side. Gavotte lay on the other side of the fire, his hands under his head. Zebbie got out his beloved old fiddle, tuned up, and played. Oustide the storm was raging, growing worse all the time. Zebbie played and played. The worse the tumult, the harder the storm, the harder he played. I remember I was holding my breath, expecting the house to be blown away every moment, and Zebbie was playing what he called "Bonaparte's Retreat." It all seemed to flash before me — I could see those poor, suffering soldiers staggering along in the snow, sacrifices to one man's unholy ambition. I verily believe we were all bewitched.

from *Letters of a Woman Homesteader* by Eleanor Pruitt Stewart. Lincoln: University of Nebraska Press, 1989. Reprinted from the 1914 original. pp. 108–111.

On the Surface

1 Who is writing the letter?

_____

2 Where and when does the evening take place?

_____

3 What events mark the evening?

_____

4 What adjectives best describe the cabin?

_____

Discoveries

1 Find out the meaning of the following words as they are used in the passage.

   a peculiar _____

   b forerunner _____

   c tumult _____

2 Colloquial language is language that is informal, for example, "critter."

   List five colloquial terms, in current use or from the past.

_____

Delving More Deeply

1   What is the purpose of this description?

_____

2   Copy three phrases which convey the comforts of Gavotte's cabin.

_____

_____

3   What impression of Gavotte does the passage convey?

_____

4   Why does the writer describe the wind as a "sighing wail"?

_____

_____

Hidden Depths

1   Describe the effect of the storm's noise and fiddle music on the writer. Then describe a time when music has affected you similarly.

_____

_____

_____

2   How are the storm and Zebbie's music linked?

_____

_____

Extend Yourself

•   Read other letters from pioneers who went west. Were their experiences like the writer's?

•   Dramatize the event told in the letter, and add scenes to it. Ask classmates to read or perform your dramatization with you.

•   Listen to recordings of folk music played on the fiddle and on other instruments pioneers had: banjos and harmonicas, for example. Write a paragraph describing the impression the music makes on you.

LESSON 13 Stand Clear

Cross-Curriculum Literacy Links: Geography; History

Text Type	Poem
Purpose	To express ideas in precise and powerful language
Structure	Stanzas
Features	Careful word choice for meaning and sound, figurative language, verse, rhyme, imagery

"Death of a Tree"

The power saw screamed
then turned to a muttering.
She leaned forward,
fell.
A sad abruptness
in the limpness of foliage,
in the final folding of limbs.
I placed my hand on what was left:
one hundred years of graceful beauty ended,
and the underside of leaves pale
blended with the morning rain.
Better for her to have been overpowered
by wind or storm.
That would have been a battle,
a fitter end for such a forest giant
than this ignoble inevitability
because man was involved.
Man is pain.
I walked away and left her,
saddened,
aware of my loss.
Yet — still,
part of the gain.

"Death of a Tree" by Jack Davis, in *Through Australian Eyes: Prose and Poetry for Schools*, Eds. John and Dorothy Colmer. Melbourne: Macmillan, 1984. p. 23.

On the Surface

1   What is the poem about?

_____

2   How old was the tree?

_____

3   How does the poet feel about the situation?

_____

4   According to the poet, what would have been a better end for the tree?

_____

5   Give one example of the way the tree is given human qualities.

_____

_____

Discoveries

1   Look up the meanings of the following words in your dictionary.

   a muttering _____

   b abruptness _____

   c inevitability _____

2   Personification involves giving inanimate objects human qualities. Write a one-paragraph description of your house using personification. For example, is it a tired house, an energetic house? Does the gate sing when you open it?

_____

_____

_____

Reading Comprehension Across the Genres 8, SV1419023632

Delving More Deeply

1 What is the effect of the title?

_____

_____

2 List words or phrases which create a mood of sadness.

_____

_____

_____

3 What is the message of the poem?

_____

_____

_____

4 What does the poet mean when he writes "Yet — still, part of the gain"?

_____

_____

_____

Hidden Depths

1 Do you believe that most people respect the environment? Give reasons for your response.

_____

_____

_____

_____

_____

_____

_____

_____

2 Write a poem about the environment. This should be ten lines. You could write about your local area, your school, or a place you feel is under threat in the world.

Extend Yourself

- Create an anthology of poems that have the environment as a theme. Illustrate these with your own drawings.

- Read more of the works of Jack Davis. Research his life and write a report.

- Find out how many kinds of products are made using timber. Present your findings in a poster or brochure.

The Middle Ages

Cross-Curriculum Literacy Links: History; Civics and Citizenship

Text Type	Report: History
Purpose	To present factual information
Structure	1 Opening — general definition
	2 Sequence of related statements about the topic
	3 Concluding statement
Features	Use of past tense, descriptive language, dates

from *A Short History of the World*

In the late Middle Ages, the spoken word was first challenged as a medium by the printing press, but it was the clock which preceded the press as a medium of influence. It could not be foreseen that in Europe a day would arrive when nearly every adult would own a clock. Early mechanical clocks carried a huge face, were hugely expensive, and were made primarily to announce the time in public places. To manufacture a clock and another innovation of the era, the military cannon, required the services of highly skilled metal workers, and indeed clockmakers were often gunmakers.

Residents of big Italian towns were the first to hear the chiming of a clock and to watch its hands move stiffly around the dial. The clock had to sit high in a tower so that people in the square and nearby streets could see its hand: usually there was an hour hand but no hand to show the minutes. Citizens might not yet be able to tell the time but at least they could nod approvingly when friends — eager to parade their knowledge — told them what the time was. Probably the first clock in Europe was installed in a large church in Milan in 1335. And the hourly sound of its bells could be heard throughout the night. In the following 20 years the northern Italian cities of Padua, Genoa and Bologna each displayed a tall public clock which chimed the hour, with one single chime announcing one o'clock and 12 chimes for midday. Paris went a step further, installing three public clocks and instructing church bellringers to watch the clocks closely and ring their bells every hour so that the entire city knew the time of day. In such cities the public clock must have been a persistent teacher of the art of counting — at least counting to the number 12 — in the centuries before education became compulsory.

These early mechanical clocks were a link between the traditional world ruled by the sun, moon and stars and a world which is now ruled by machines. Some big clocks provided knowledge which the booming profession of astrology required for its forecasting. The clock on the cathedral at Strasbourg displayed from about the 1350s a dial on which the positions of sun, moon and the main planets were indicated. The exact relationship between these heavenly bodies was a vital recipe for predicting when tasks and enterprises should be begun, indeed a guide to predicting the destiny of each individual. That a cathedral should combine faith in Christ and faith in the stars was not seen as heretical.

Strasbourg's clock was perhaps the most complicated machine of any kind seen in the world so far, but it was not yet accurate. The margin of error in a public clock could be as large as 15 minutes in a day, and therefore the clock required a skilled attendant to correct the time with regularity. Little by little the mechanism and accuracy of the clock was refined. By the early 1600s, rich merchants were buying expensive clocks for the walls of their own houses, and the city of Augsburg in southern Germany employed 43 master clockmakers as well as their assistants. Half a century later the master mechanic Christiaan Huygens introduced the pendulum to the clock, and cut the margin of error to about 10 seconds in every 24 hours.

from *A Short History of the World* by Geoffrey Blainey. Melbourne: Penguin, 2000. pp. 284–5.

On the Surface

1   In addition to the clock, what was the medium of influence in the Middle Ages?

_____

2   Why were there so few clocks in the Middle Ages?

_____

3   Where were the first clocks in Europe? _____

4   What did the clock teach citizens? _____

5   What was the margin of error in early clocks? _____

Discoveries

1   Find out the meanings of the following words.

a   foreseen _____

b   innovation _____

c   heretical _____

2   The third person is often used for report writing, as in this excerpt. Write about the installation of the town clock in the first person from the point of view of a villager who has just learned how to tell the time. (50 words)

_____

_____

_____

_____

_____

_____

Delving More Deeply

1   Explain what is meant by the clocks being a link between the traditional world ruled by the sun and a world which is now ruled by machines.

_____

_____

_____

2   What role do you think the town square played in people's live in the Middle Ages?

_____

3   When was the pendulum clock introduced? _____

4   What would have been the impact of the printing press?

_____

Hidden Depths

1   To what extent is your world ruled by the clock?

_____

_____

2   List three inventions that have occurred in your lifetime and briefly explain their impact.

_____

_____

_____

_____

Extend Yourself

•   Find out when digital clocks came into common use. Discuss with classmates whether digital or analog (dial) clocks are easier to use, and why.

•   Write a 500-word report on how to make better use of your time.

•   Create a daily and weekly planner page, make copies for your class, and demonstrate how to use it for your classmates.

•   Invent something that will save time. Present it to the class as a poster.

LESSON 15 **Another Continent**

Cross-Curriculum Literacy Links: Geography; Multicultural Content

Text Type	Map
Purpose	To show locations and physical features
Structure	1 Pictorial representations of a region
	2 Scale and Introduction are often shown
Features	Visual information; combining words, symbols and images; scale; key

South America

Reading Comprehension Across the Genres 8, SV1419023632

South America

South America is a region of immense variety and beauty. The archaeological remains of ancient civilizations can be found among its jungles and mountains. Geographically there are three main regions: the immense mountain range of the Andes; the central, vast river basins; and the geologically ancient northern Guiana Highlands and Brazilian Highlands.

The highest navigable lake in the world is found in the Andes on the border of Peru and Bolivia, and the largest tropical rainforest in the world can be found in the Amazon Basin. In the north of Chile the Atacama Desert contains some of the driest places on earth. Parts of the desert have been without rain for 400 years.

Lake Titicaca

Lake Titicaca in Bolivia is the highest navigable lake in the world. This huge inland sea was once at the centre of Tiahuanaco civilization, and near the southeast end of the lake can be seen the ruins of the Gate of the Sun, once part of an elaborate conservatory and courtyard built by a civilization that surfaced around 6000 BC and disappeared around AD 1200.

from *Traveller's Atlas of the World*. New Lanark: Geddes & Grosset, 2000. p. 27.

On the Surface

1   What is the largest country in South America?

_____

2   Which countries are on the equator?

_____

3   What is the capital of Argentina?

_____

4   Which oceans surround the continent?

_____

Discoveries

1   What symbol is used to indicate major cities and towns? _____

2   Design the symbols needed for a map of your school or local area.

Reading Comprehension Across the Genres 8, SV1419023632

Delving More Deeply

1 Which country has control of the Falkland Islands?

_____

2 In which country is Lake Titicaca?

_____

3 Which continent is South America connected to?

_____

4 Which countries would be the warmest and why?

_____

_____

_____

Hidden Depths

1 Why are the Falkland Islands famous?

_____

_____

2 What language is primarily spoken in South America?

_____

_____

Extend Yourself

- Research one of the following aspects of South America and present a two-minute talk to the class.
    — the Incas
    — the Andes
    — the Amazon rain forest
- Which countries would you like to know more about? Do you think you are well informed about the geography of South America? Why or why not?
- Prepare a brochure for a travel agent to persuade Americans to travel to South America.
- On a world map, color in all the Spanish-speaking countries.

The Numbers Game

Cross-Curriculum Literacy Links: Mathematics; Civics and Citizenship

Text Type	Graph
Purpose	Visual communication of information: a survey about an upcoming event
Structure	Bar graph of a survey, labelled x and y axes
Features	Statistics, scale can alter impact of information

Campus Chat

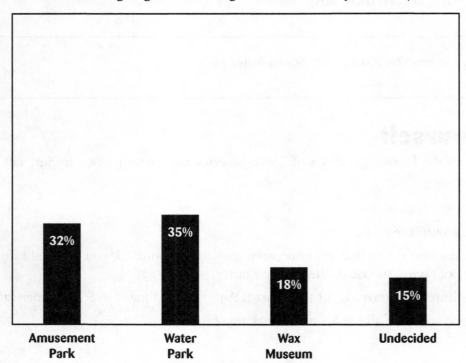

Yesterday's Results

Where do eighth graders want to go for the end-of-the-year field trip?

32%	35%	18%	15%
Amusement Park	Water Park	Wax Museum	Undecided

Total votes: 237, representing 85% of all eighth graders

On the Surface

1   What kind of graph is this?

_____

2   What is the size of the sample?

_____

3   What percentage voted for the trip to the water park?

_____

4   How many people voted for the wax museum?

_____

5   What number would constitute about 50 percent of the sample?

_____

Discoveries

1   One bar of the graph is captioned as "undecided." What can you assume about the voters represented by this bar?

_____

2   Why do captions and labels on graphs need to be simple and brief?

_____

Delving More Deeply

1   Is this sample a reliable indicator of students' wishes?

_____

_____

2   Why would a school conduct this poll?

_____

3   If school staff uses this poll, where will students go on their end-of-the-year field trip?

_____

Hidden Depths

1 35% of students voted to go to the water park. 32% voted to go to the amusement park. How can they decide which place to visit?

_____

_____

2 What polls have you heard or read about lately? What is the function of polls?

_____

_____

_____

Extend Yourself

• Survey your class on this issue and graph the results.

• Design a different kind of graph to represent the same information. Discuss with classmates how the graphs differ and which is easier to read.

• Locate and bring in graphs from magazines and newspapers. Display these and discuss how they present information.

A New Mammal

Cross-Curriculum Literacy Links: History; Science

Text Type	Explanation
Purpose	To explain why things are as they are
Structure	1 A general statement
	2 Series of events in chronological or logical order
	3 Concluding statement
Features	Logical sequence of details or ideas

Hello, My Possum

The city of Victoria in Australia is home to the world's latest-discovered mammal — a possum plagued by a 170-year-old case of mistaken identity.

Until recently, the mountain brushtail species was thought to be the same as possums in parts of New South Wales and Queensland.

Dr. David Lindenmayer, an associate professor of ecology at Australian National University, came across differences while helping his wife, Karen Viggers, complete her PhD. They were measuring and observing possums in Victoria, NSW, and Queensland.

With the help of ANU statistician Ross Cunningham — after whom the new species, *trichosaurus cunninghamii* is named — Dr. Lindenmayer's suspicions were proved correct late last year.

"The discovery of a species was not my main game. It was a side adventure that turned out to be quite exciting," Dr. Lindenmayer said.

"It's a rare thing to discover a new mammal.

"It took a few years for genetic tests to 100 percent confirm the finding.

"We now have two different species. This means there's still a lot to learn about mammals in Victoria.

"Australia is a lot more diverse than we previously thought and that's exciting."

To the untrained eye, the differences between the mountain brushtail species in Victoria and parts of southern NSW and Queensland are slight.

Dr. Lindenmayer said it was no wonder the Victorian species had not been identified in about 170 years.

"The average punter[1] couldn't tell the difference," he said. "This shows there's a lot more happening with our mammals than we thought."

He said the two species had identical body shapes and weight, but the Victorian possums had larger ears, longer feet and shorter tails. The Victorian species also had a flatter face — the short-eared variety tended to have fox-like features.

Dr. Lindenmayer said the brushtail possum lived in wet forest areas, including parts of Marysville, Healesville and Gippsland.

Dr. Lindenmayer said the exciting discovery highlighted the importance of preserving Australian wildlife.

"As custodians of the land, we have to do better," he said.

"There is a need to think more carefully about better forest management to conserve native animals and to ensure undiscovered species are not missed because poor management has wiped them out."

"Hello, my possum," by Mary Papadakis. *Sunday Herald Sun*, 12 January 2003, p. 7.

[1]someone hunting from a shallow boat propelled by a long pole

On the Surface

1 What is the newly discovered mammal? What is its exact name?

_____

2 Why has it only been recently discovered?

_____

3 Who made the discovery?

_____

4 How was the existence of a separate species proved?

_____

Discoveries

1 Find out the meanings of the following words.

   a plagued _____

   b custodians _____

   c diverse _____

2 Some words in the text use hyphens, such as "fox-like" and "short-eared." Hyphens create a link between words that go together. Rewrite the sentences below, adding hyphens where you think they are needed.

   a Max is studying hard for his end of year exams.

_____

   b The bell shaped cage was certainly the most unusual.

_____

Delving More Deeply

1   What is the difference between NSW possums and Victorian possums?

_____

_____

2   What did Dr Lindenmayer mean when he said that "As custodians of the land, we have to do better"? Do you agree with him?

_____

_____

3   What environment is favored by the mountain brushtail possum?

_____

4   What is ecology?

_____

Hidden Depths

1   Do you think this is a significant discovery? Explain.

_____

_____

2   How are you a custodian of the environment? Explain the ways you help to look after the environment every day.

_____

_____

Extend Yourself

• Write a leaflet for tourists that explains the differences between the NSW possum and the Victorian possum.

• Write a children's story introducing the new possum.

• Research an extinct animal and write a poem about it.

A Long Walk

Cross-Curriculum Literacy Links: History; Work, Employment and Enterprise

Text Type	Narrative
Purpose	To tell a story
Structure	1 Introduction — who, what, where and when
	2 Complication
	3 Series of events
	4 Resolution
Features	Description, characterization, dialogue

from *Life in the Iron Mills*

"Where are ye goin', Deb? The rain's sharp."

"To the mill, with Hugh's supper."

"Let him bide till th' morn. Sit ye down."

"No, no," — sharply pushing her off. "The boy'll starve."

She hurried from the cellar, while the child wearily coiled herself up for sleep. The rain was falling heavily, as the woman, pail in hand, emerged from the mouth of the alley, and turned down the narrow street, that stretched out, long and black, miles before her. Here and there a flicker of gas lighted an uncertain space of muddy footwalk and gutter; the long rows of houses, except an occasional lager-bier shop, were closed; now and then she met a band of mill-hands skulking to or from their work.

Not many even of the inhabitants of a manufacturing town know the vast machinery of system by which the bodies of workmen are governed, that goes on unceasingly from year to year. The hands of each mill are divided into watches that relieve each other as regularly as the sentinels of an army. By night and day the work goes on, the unsleeping engines groan and shriek, the fiery pools of metal boil and surge. Only for a day in the week, in half-courtesy to public censure, the fires are partially veiled; but as soon as the clock strikes midnight, the great furnaces break forth with renewed fury, the clamor begins with fresh, breathless vigor, the engines sob and shriek like "gods in pain."

As Deborah hurried down through the heavy rain, the noise of these thousand engines sounded through the sleep and shadow of the city like far-off thunder. The mill to which she was going lay on the river, a mile below the city-limits. It was far, and she was weak, aching from standing twelve hours at the spools. Yet it was her almost nightly walk to take this man his supper, though at every square she sat down to rest, and she knew she should receive small word of thanks. . . .

The road leading to the mills had been quarried from the solid rock, which rose abrupt and bare on one side on the cinder-covered road, while the river, sluggish and black, crept past on the other. The mills for rolling iron are simply immense tent-like roofs, covering acres of ground, open on every side. Beneath these roofs Deborah looked in on a city of fires, that burned hot and fiercely in the night. Fire in every horrible form: pits of flame waving in the wind; liquid metal-flames writhing in tortuous streams through the sand; wide cauldrons filled with boiling fire, over which bent ghastly wretches stirring the strange brewing; and through all, crowds of half-clad men, looking like revengeful ghosts in the red light, hurried, throwing masses of glittering fire. It was like a street in Hell. Even Deborah muttered, as she crept through, "'T looks like t' Devil's place!" It did, — in more ways than one.

She found the man she was looking for, at last, heaping coal on a furnace. He had not time to eat his supper; . . . Deborah was stupid with sleep; her back pained her sharply; and her teeth chattered with cold, with the rain that soaked her clothes and dripped from her at every step. She stood, however, patiently holding the pail, and waiting.

from *Life in the Iron Mills and Other Stories* by Rebecca Harding Davis. New York: CUNY Press, 1985. Originally published in 1861. pp. 18–20.

On the Surface

1 What are the mills that figure so largely in this passage?

_____

2 Who makes the long journey through the rain, and why?

_____

3 What is the name of the man she is going to see?

_____

4 What forces hinder Deborah in her journey?

_____

_____

Discoveries

1 Define these words from the passage.

a skulking _____

b sentinels _____

c censure _____

d stupid _____

2 What do the opening lines of dialogue hint about the social standing of Deb and the person who tells her to stay in?

_____

_____

_____

Delving More Deeply

1   On what contrasting images does the passage rely?

2   Workers in the factories were called "hands." What does this say about their role in the mills?

3   What impression does the narrator give of the town and its inhabitants?

4   After giving Hugh his dinner, Deborah falls asleep on a slag heap of iron. What does this tell us about her?

Hidden Depths

1   Why does Deborah make this terrible journey almost every night? What makes you say so?

2   What hazards do the "crowds of half-clad men" face while working in the iron mills? How do you think the narrator feels about them?

Extend Yourself

•   Do some research into the Industrial Revolution. What great changes did it bring? What problems came along with it? Write a report for your classmates.

•   Visit a steel mill, or read about what steel mills are like today. Share photos and videos with your classmates. Discuss how conditions and safety standards have changed.

•   Read *Life in the Iron Mills* to find out what happens to Hugh and Deborah, and write a review for your classmates.

•   Draw or paint the iron mill, based on the description in the passage.

Reading Comprehension Across the Genres 8, SV1419023632

Text Type	Advertisement
Purpose	To persuade people to purchase a product
Structure	Images and words
Features	Persuasive words, may include images, facts, logical reasoning, examples

Historical Advertisement

Now's the time for JELL-O

Having a little trouble, Mac? Buck up! You still can surprise the little woman and the kids with a swell Jell-O gelatin dessert! It's an absolute cinch to make . . . and we guarantee they'll love every bit of it!

JELL-O IS A REGISTERED TRADE-MARK OF GENERAL FOODS CORP.

Copr. 1952, General Foods Corp.

On the Surface

1 What product is being advertised?

_____

2 Who is the intended audience for this advertisement?

_____

_____

3 What, according to this advertisement, are the advantages of this product?

_____

4 List the colloquialisms (slang).

_____

_____

Discoveries

1 This advertisement uses contractions (eg., we've) to make it sound like spoken language. Write out all the contractions in this advertisement in full.

_____

2 The word *little* is used twice in this advertisement. Explain the meaning of *little* in each usage.

_____

_____

_____

Delving More Deeply

1 When do you think this advertisement was produced?

_____

2 List three clues that lead you to this conclusion.

_____

_____

3 What assumptions does this advertisement make about men of that time?

_____

_____

4 What assumptions does this advertisement make about women of that time?

_____

_____

Hidden Depths

1 To what extent do you think this advertisement would be successful in persuading men of today to make this product?

_____

_____

_____

2 Do you think advertising has created too many negative stereotypes of men?

_____

_____

_____

_____

Extend Yourself

• Write a set of guidelines to avoid stereotyping in advertising.

• In pairs, choose a small selection of advertisements from one popular women's magazine. Each pair should cover a different magazine. How do they portray women? What do the advertisements tell you about the intended audience? Present your findings to the class.

• Rewrite this advertisement for today's audience and suggest accompanying artwork.

Reading Comprehension Across the Genres 8, SV1419023632

LESSON 20 Ring, Ring

Cross-Curriculum Literacy Links: Science; Technology

Text Type	Argument
Purpose	To put forward an argument
Structure	**1** Point of view stated
	2 Justifications of argument in a logical order
	3 Summing up of argument
Features	Includes facts and figures, logical reasoning, examples, persuasive or emotive language

Mobile Mania

The current craze for cell phones is ridiculous! Think about it: How many of your family, friends, and acquaintances do not have one? Can you think of anyone? While there are many good reasons for having a mobile phone, these are not always valid. Parents who are worried about their children may give their offspring a phone so that they can be contacted in case of an emergency. And of course, those who are in business need them for work. However, most cell phones are unnecessary.

Do you really need to IM your friend at all hours of the day? It seems we can never stop communicating, with some users phoning to announce their imminent arrival. Who needs those corny ring tones and diabolical ditties punctuating the day?

Worst of all, how many of us have sat staring into space while our companion has an enthusiastic conversation with their cell phone?

The biggest argument against cell phones is the cost. Many young people are struggling to pay back colossal debts before they even have a full-time job! Land line phones are cheaper. Perhaps this mobile mania has been caused by all that radiation emitted from the handsets.

On the Surface

1 What is the writer's contention (main point)?

_____

2 List the arguments for cell phones.

_____

3 List the arguments against cell phones.

_____

_____

4 What is the effect of the heading, "Mobile mania"?

_____

5 What suggestions are made in the final paragraph?

_____

_____

Discoveries

1 Write the meanings of the following words.

   a imminent _____

   b diabolical _____

   c emit _____

   d mania _____

2 **a** List at least ten text messaging abbreviations.

   _____   _____

   _____   _____

   _____   _____

   _____   _____

   _____   _____

   b Write a brief message using some of the abbreviations.

   _____

   c Rewrite the message in standard English.

   _____

Delving More Deeply

1 List examples of loaded language in this argument (i.e., language that has positive or negative associations — emotive, powerful language).

_____

_____

2 Give an example of a rhetorical question (a question that suggests its own answer) from the passage.

_____

_____

_____

3 Give an example of the rude behavior displayed by some cell phone users.

_____

_____

4 Which business people would especially depend on mobile phones? Give three examples.

_____

Hidden Depths

1 Do you think the writer's argument is persuasive? Would it appeal to some people but not others? Which people? Why? Give reasons for your answer.

_____

_____

_____

2 Can you think of any other reasons for cell phones?

_____

_____

Extend Yourself

• Write your own 250-word argument that advocates the wide use of cell phones. Aim to include some of the following persuasive techniques: statistics, appeals, loaded language.

• The title is an example of alliteration (the repetition of consonants, in this case, the letter m). Scan through magazines and newspapers to find other examples. Why do writers use it?

• Write a story in which a character does not have a cell phone. How does this cause problems or create advantages?

LESSON 21 # Fast Food

Cross-Curriculum Literacy Links: Technology, Science

Text Type	Instructions, procedure
Purpose	To give instructions or show how something is accomplished through a series of steps
Structure	1 Opening statement of goal or aim
	2 Series of steps listed in chronological order
Features	Logical sequence of steps; may use technical language and diagrams

How to Use Your New MicroPro Deluxe Microwave

Using the Timer Use the built-in timer to monitor the cooking process.

- Push Timer.
- Enter the time in minutes and seconds using the number pad.
- Then press Start. The timer will beep when the time has expired. Note that this timer does not shut off the oven.

Using the MicroTime Feature MicroTime allows you to microwave for a set amount of time. Use this feature for regular microwave cooking.

- Place the food or beverage on the turntable. Push MicroTime.
- Enter the time to cook in minutes and seconds using the number pad.
- Push Power Level and select a power from 1 (low) to 10 (high).
- Then press Start. When the time has expired, the oven will stop and display "Done."

Important Safety Precautions Read and understand these precautions.

- Do not heat closed jars or tightly sealed containers.
- Cookware may become very hot; use potholders.
- Liquids may start to boil; stir the liquid before removing it from the oven.
- Hot foods may have steam. When opening bags or containers of food, direct the steam away from your face and hands.

Service Qualified technicians are ready to help at a Service Center near you.

- First refer to the Trouble Shooting section of this manual (p. 87). Look for a description of your problem.
- If you still have a problem, call 1-800-555-OVEN for the nearest Service Center.

On the Surface

1   What is the main purpose of this selection?

_____

2   This selection is arranged into four categories. What are they, and how do you know?

_____

_____

3   What number should be called if a repair is needed?

_____

4   What is the highest power setting for the microwave?

_____

5   Under which category do you find bulleted items that do not need to be completed in order?

_____

_____

Discoveries

1   Write the basic meaning for each word as it is used in the selection. Then below the meaning, write a new sentence using the word.

   a   monitor: _____

_____

   b   expired: _____

_____

   c   technician: _____

_____

2   What is the name on each button of the microwave? How do you know?

_____

_____

_____

Delving More Deeply

1 Does this microwave have a turntable? What is the purpose of a turntable?

_____

_____

2 Review the safety precautions. Then answer the following questions.

a Why do you think closed jars and sealed containers should not be heated?

_____

b What do you think might happen if you do not stir the boiling liquid before removing the dish?

_____

3 What is the basic difference between the regular timer and the MicroTime feature?

_____

Hidden Depths

1 Why are product manuals important?

_____

_____

_____

2 What does a product manual need in order to be really useful?

_____

_____

Extend Yourself

• Make up a crazy new product. Then write a brief product manual for it.

• Find an old product manual that contains a set of instructions in step-by-step (chronological) order. Cut up the instructions so that each step is on its own strip. Then scramble the strips and challenge a friend to put them back in the right order.

• As a class, search through magazines or newspapers, identifying as many sets of instructions or how-to articles as possible. Then work together to rank them from best (clearest and most useful) to worst.

LESSON 22 The Woes of Shopping

Cross-Curriculum Literacy Links: Science; Geography; Civics and Citizenship

Text Type	Discussion
Purpose	To present information and opinions about more than one side of an issue
Structure	1 Opening statement presenting the issue
	2 Arguments or evidence for different points of view
	3 Concluding recommendation
Features	Includes facts and figures, logical reasoning, examples, persuasive or emotive language

Plastic Bags

Should there be a fee for plastic shopping bags?

Put your hand up if you have a secret stash of plastic shopping bags. We all do because we collect them every week, some of us every day.

There are many obvious reasons we should charge a fee for shopping bags. Despite the fact that we are all aware of the damage plastic does to the environment, Americans still collect huge numbers of shopping bags as they stroll through department stores or struggle home with the weekly shopping. Billions of them per year, in fact! The person who comes armed with his own environmentally friendly reusable bag is a rarity. The time has come to be tough. If we start charging 25 cents each for these bags, there will be far less enthusiasm for them. This has been proved overseas. In Ireland a fee was charged for plastic bags, and this reduced bag usage by 90 per cent!

We are a society that loves convenience, and we will have to train ourselves to plan ahead when we go shopping by taking the appropriate bags if we wish to avoid being charged. This seems a small sacrifice if it means saving the environment.

However, there is another factor to be considered. If the fee were to be introduced, there would be several hundred jobs lost in the plastics industry. This argument ignores the fact that jobs would be created in administering the fee and for companies that wish to manufacture reusable cloth shopping bags.

Perhaps the most persuasive image of all is the sorry sight of a twisted plastic bag polluting the local lake. The government must not be lazy about the fee.

On the Surface

1 Why do Americans have so many plastic bags?

_____

2 What is the proposed fee?

_____

3 How many bags do Americans use per year?

_____

4 What was the result of Ireland's shopping bag fee?

_____

5 List one argument against the fee.

_____

Discoveries

1 Find the meanings of the following words as they are used in the text.

   a fee _____

   b rarity _____

   c administering _____

2 The subjunctive mood is used when an action is not asserted but is rather only suggested, wished, doubted, or feared, for example, "If the fee were to be introduced, there would. . . ." The writer could have avoided the subjunctive by saying, "If the fee is introduced, there will. . . ." Why do you think subjunctive mood is used in the article?

_____

_____

3 Which of the following sentences are in the subjunctive mood?

   a I would not go to that party if I were you.

   b Smoking should be banned in all public places.

   c He behaves as if he owned the street!

Delving More Deeply

1 Why does the writer include statistics?

_____

2 Why does the writer use "we" in the argument?

_____

3 Why do you think the writer ended with the image of the plastic bag?

_____

4 Why does the writer include the arguments against the fee?

_____

_____

5 How could the writer have made the piece more persuasive?

_____

_____

Hidden Depths

1 Do you agree with the fee, or are there other ways to reduce plastic bag usage?

_____

_____

2 Which other non-essential items do we use daily or weekly which harm the environment? What are some alternatives to these?

_____

_____

Extend Yourself

• Investigate your home for throw-away products and excessive packaging. Make a list of these environmentally unfriendly products, and suggest ways to reduce people's reliance on them.

• Create a poster or a website to promote the idea that people should not rely on plastic bags.

LESSON 23 # Too Much TV?

Cross-Curriculum Literacy Links: Science; Geography; Arts

Text Type	Cartoon
Purpose	To comment on an issue
Structure	Picture with caption
Features	Caricatures, dialogue, humor; may be related to current affairs or social issues

Playground Tribes

On the Surface

1 Describe the cartoon's setting.

_____

2 Who is the adult with the children?

_____

3 How are the children portrayed?

_____

4 What is the adult holding, and what is its purpose?

_____

Discoveries

1 Define "satire."

_____

_____

2 Explain how satire is different from other types of comedy.

_____

_____

Delving More Deeply

1 What issue is the cartoon satirizing?

_____

_____

2 To what extent do you need to have prior knowledge of the issue to understand the cartoon?

_____

_____

_____

3 Why is the adult's speech to the children funny? Why is it ridiculous in this setting?

_____

_____

_____

4 Who is ridiculed as watching too much TV? How do you know?

_____

_____

_____

Hidden Depths

1 To what extent do cartoonists rely on humor? Are there some issues that should not be treated humorously? Explain.

_____

_____

2 Are cartoonists able to make comments that writers may not? If you were a cartoonist, which issues would you consider portraying? Why?

_____

_____

Extend Yourself

• Collect a series of cartoons from a major newspaper for a week. Which issues were covered? What devices did cartoonists use to make their points?

• Draw a cartoon satirizing an issue you consider important.

• Research the issue of "too much TV." How much TV does the average eighth grader watch? How much is too much? Arrange a debate in your class: Students should or should not watch TV on school nights.

• In cartoons, a caricature is an exaggeration of a person's features or qualities. For example, a politician may be drawn with his or her facial features emphasized in a dramatic way with a large chin or heavy eyebrows. Find examples of caricatures in recent cartoons and explain what they show about the person caricatured.

LESSON 24 Music for Everyone

Cross-Curriculum Literacy Links: Science; Arts

Text Type	Newspaper article
Purpose	To offer the reader an account of current affairs and issues at a local, national, and global level
Structure	1 Detailed information
	2 Headline
	3 By-line — states the name of the journalist and other details
	4 A general statement: most important details are offered first
	5 Series of short paragraphs
	6 Concluding statement
Features	Most of the text consists of facts, logical sequence of ideas, reported speech, objective language

Does Music Matter?

Schools May Be Making Unwise Cuts

By Junie Serenada, Youth Affairs Reporter

With schools around the nation facing stricter standardized tests, schedules are squeezed for every minute of study time. Some schools have cut back on recess, lunch time, and PE. Others are letting arts classes slip. However, there is evidence cutting music classes does more harm than good.

Preliminary research suggests that learning music, participating in making music, and listening to music can strengthen students academically. Why is this?

First, studying an instrument, including voice, builds stamina and discipline. Students who learn to concentrate through progressively longer practice sessions can transfer this ability to other studies. Concentration is a must when testing as well.

Second, proficiency in music and proficiency in mathematics seem to be statistically linked. Some studies show that students who are involved in music — band, choir, or orchestra — have higher levels of math ability through twelfth grade. And the more years of music, the more increase in math skills.

When it comes to testing, student-musicians also seem to have an edge, scoring higher on both sections of the SAT than their music-deprived colleagues. Music students more often make honor roll and receive academic honors, in comparison with students who don't study music.

These are early findings, and experts don't have all the answers about why studying music helps

students succeed in academics and testing. However, research into music's effect on the brain is underway. Using functional magnetic resource imaging (MRI), scientists are detecting differences in the brains of people who study music. Performing music seems to initiate activity in all four of the cortex's lobes and in parts of the cerebellum, leading to greater dexterity and increased spatial reasoning.

The jury's still out on what's going on in the brain when a boy practices cello or a girl sight-reads a new piano piece. But there is enough evidence to suggest that cutting back on music to boost academic achievement is an unwise move.

On the Surface

1   Why are some schools cutting back on recess, PE, and arts classes?

_____

2   What is the writer's opinion about these cuts?

_____

3   What impression is created by the headline?

_____

4   In what academic subject is music study apparently most helpful?

_____

Discoveries

1   Define these words as they are used in the article.

   a   stamina _____

   b   a must _____

   c   colleagues _____

2   List the three abbreviations that occur in the article. What do these stand for?

_____

_____

Delving More Deeply

Considering the article, tell whether the statements are true or false.

1   Research definitely shows studying music makes you smarter. _____

2   Music is too difficult for children to study. _____

3   Scientists have no idea how music affects the brain. _____

4 The arguments used to support the idea that music matters are that:

a proficiency in music and math seem to be linked _____

b most children already study music in school _____

c music teaches concentration skills _____

d music students more often make the honor roll _____

Hidden Depths

1 What do you think about cutting music and other arts classes in favor of more time for test prep? Why?

_____

_____

_____

2 What extra-curricular (non-academic) activities do you participate in? Have they affected your academic performance? If so, how?

_____

_____

_____

Extend Yourself

• Hold a class debate on whether cuts to non-academic programs help or harm students.

• Use the Internet to find out what new research shows about the brain and music. Present your findings to the class.

• Collect quotes about the importance of music in people's lives. Make a booklet that combines quotes and images of music and musicians.

• Invite a musician to talk to the class about how music has affected his or her life.

LESSON 25 Clever Pets

Cross-Curriculum Literacy Link: Science

Text Type	Magazine article
Purpose	To inform and entertain
Structure	1 Introduction
	2 Explanation
	3 Conclusion
Features	May explore a topic in some detail, may include comments from experts and technical terms. There is the space to explore ideas, not just report them.

How Do Pets Know When We Are Sick or Sad?

by Lyndal Kelley

My interest in how pets seem aware of human moods and illnesses stems from a time when I was seriously ill and my dog was unbelievably loyal and protective of me. For one year I was bedridden with severe muscular pain and Ashley, my Bichon x Shih Tzu cross, stayed on my bed beside me for hours on end. Even people he knew well he no longer trusted fully around me while I was in such a vulnerable state.

It is not just that pets seem to understand when someone is sick or sad, but that they empathize as well. They want to help and comfort. Dogs often show concern in their eyes for a sick person and stay close by. Veterinarian Dr. Geoff Hayres says pheromones (scent hormones) may explain how dogs and cats sense when someone is sick or feeling low in their mood. Pheromones are secreted by humans and many animals and are thought to trigger a variety of instinctive behaviors.

One example of pheromones is that pets seem to understand death better when they are allowed to sniff the body of the deceased. Dr. Hayres says that early in his career an elderly couple with two poodles came to him when one of their dogs was very sick. It had to be put to sleep and the other poodle was not present at the time. The remaining poodle spent the next few years searching for its mate, especially when they went to their vacation house. It was this experience that led Dr. Hayres to believe that by smelling the deceased body, an animal can understand that its friend is not coming back.

Both dogs and cats observe their owners carefully and adapt their own behavior accordingly. Animal behaviorist and veterinarian Dr. Robert Holmes says he is not convinced that pets cognitively know when someone is sick, but rather they respond to a change in their body language. Dogs have been known to predict when a person is about to have a seizure. This is most likely due to the animal observing some kind of change in body language, or detecting an odor undetectable to the human nose, that the body gives off prior to a seizure.

My family has a three-year-old miniature Schnauzer called Brock, who can be somewhat excitable, especially when he sees other dogs. However, when we take him into my nanna's nursing home he becomes very gentle. He loves sitting on nanna's knee and on her bed, and has been quite protective of her corner of the room. He loves the attention he receives from other residents and will even sit on their knees in their wheelchairs. Whether Brock observes the frail body language of the residents or smells some kind of bodily scent, his perfect behavior in the nursing home has certainly surprised us.

Pets n People Magazine,
vol. 4, issue 23, 2002, p. 72.

81

On the Surface

1   Why did the writer become interested in how pets seem aware of human moods and illnesses?

_____

2   How do dogs show concern?

_____

3   When do animals understand death better?

_____

4   How can dogs predict when someone is about to have a seizure?

_____

5   What change did the writer observe in her dog when she took him to the nursing home?

_____

Discoveries

Write the meanings of the following words as they are used in the text.

1   vulnerable _____

2   empathize _____

3   secreted _____

4   cognitively _____

Delving More Deeply

1   What are pheromones?

_____

2   How do you know that this is a magazine article rather than a newspaper article? Describe the differences.

_____

_____

3 Why do you think the writer included a reference to Dr. Robert Holmes and other experts in the piece?

_____

4 What kind of audience would enjoy this article?

_____

Hidden Depths

1 Have you ever had or known of a pet that could empathize with a person's moods? Tell the story.

_____

_____

_____

2 a What role might pets have in the recovery of humans?

_____

_____

b Which jobs and people rely on dogs? Why?

_____

_____

_____

Extend Yourself

- This writer has used a series of personal anecdotes to illustrate the topic. This is an effective technique to make magazine writing more interesting. Imagine you had to write an article about buying a dog. Write the opening paragraph of the article using an anecdote.

- Write a magazine article on a topic of your choice. You must select a particular magazine and topic. It could be a teen, sports, or current affairs magazine.

- Use one of the following techniques to make the opening of your piece more interesting: statistics, an anecdote, a question or a surprising fact or statement.

At the Gym

Cross-Curriculum Literacy Links: PE; Health; Work, Employment, and Enterprise

Text Type	Timetable
Purpose	To provide information about exercise class times
Structure	Grid with times, class types, and instructor's names
Features	Abbreviations, jargon, grid format

Jim's Gym

Hours: Monday to Friday 6:00 A.M.–10:00 P.M.
Saturdays and Sundays 8:00 A.M.–7:30 P.M.

Workout timetable

TIME	MON	TUES	WED	THUR	FRI	SAT	SUN
6:30	STEP Jo	PUMP Chris	SPIN David	STEP Jo	PUMP Chris		
9:00						Hi-NRG Jenny	STEP Jo
9:30	PILATES Karen	SCULPT Kevin	YOGA Bill	STEP Jim	PILATES Karen		
10:00						PUMP Jim	PUMP Jim
10:30							
11:00							
12:00	STEP Jim		STEP Jim		STEP Jim	PILATES Karen	
1:00							
4:00							
5:00					PUMP Phil	STEP Phil	
6:00	Hi-NRG Lyn	CXT Janice	Hi-NRG Lyn	CXT Janice	YOGA Bill		STEP David
7:00	SPIN David	SPIN David	SPIN David	SPIN David			
8:00	YOGA Gerry	YOGA Gerry	YOGA Gerry	YOGA Gerry			

NOTE
All classes last for 60 minutes.
You must bring a water bottle to class.

CLASS CODES

CXT	Cross-training: a range of aerobic moves emphasizing cardiovascular fitness
STEP	Basic step moves with an emphasis on endurance
PUMP	Exercise class with weights
Hi-NRG	High-energy aerobics with some challenging choreography
PILATES	Exercise to develop posture and stability
SCULPT	Stretching exercise to tone abs
SPIN	A group exercise class on stationary bikes
YOGA	This class concludes with 15 minutes of meditation

On the Surface

1 How long are the classes?

_____

2 How many classes are held on Saturdays?

_____

3 What are the gym's hours on weekdays?

_____

4 Which class is the most frequently held at this gym? Which class is the least frequently held?

_____

5 How many different instructors teach classes at this gym? List them.

_____

_____

Discoveries

1 Look up and write out the meaning of the following terms.

   a endurance _____

   b emphasis _____

   c energy _____

2 Motivational speakers use language in a particular way to inspire people, including the use of words with positive associations (connotations). For example, instead of focusing on problems, they encourage listeners to overcome obstacles. Write a paragraph that will motivate people to exercise. Underline all the words that have positive connotations.

_____

_____

_____

Delving More Deeply

1   Why do you think there are no classes in the early afternoon?

_____

_____

2   What features might Jim's Gym offer in addition to exercise classes?

_____

3   Why would you need to bring a water bottle to class?

_____

4   Why do you think the Hi-NRG class description mentions the fact that it includes "challenging choreography"?

_____

_____

_____

Hidden Depths

1   What are the benefits of regular exercise?

_____

_____

2   What is your school's policy on physical education? Do you agree with it?

_____

_____

_____

Extend Yourself

•   Create an exercise program for yourself.

•   Research careers in the health and fitness industry and create a poster for your school's careers department.

•   Write an introductory description of Pilates or yoga.

•   Create a brochure advertising Jim's Gym.

•   Design a questionnaire about exercise habits.

NAME _____   DATE _____

LESSON 27 Dr. Frankenstein Tells All

Cross-Curriculum Literacy Link: Gender

Text Type	Narrative, novel
Purpose	To entertain and explore ideas
Structure	1 Beginning
	2 Conflict or problem
	3 Resolution
Features	Dialogue, limited character development, one main conflict

from *Frankenstein; or, The Modern Prometheus*

It was on a dreary night of November, that I beheld the accomplishment of my toils. With an anxiety that almost amounted to agony, I collected the instruments of life around me, that I might infuse a spark of being into the lifeless thing that lay at my feet. It was already one in the morning; the rain pattered dismally against the panes, and my candle was nearly burnt out, when, by the glimmer of the half-extinguished light, I saw the dull yellow eye of the creature open; it breathed hard, and a convulsive motion agitated its limbs.

How can I describe my emotions at this catastrophe, or how delineate the wretch whom with such infinite pains and care I had endeavoured to form? His limbs were in proportion, and I had selected his features as beautiful. Beautiful! — Great God! His yellow skin scarcely covered the work of muscles and arteries beneath; his hair was of a lustrous black and flowing; his teeth of a pearly whiteness; but these luxuriances only formed a more horrid contrast with his watery eyes, that seemed almost of the same colour as the dun white sockets in which they were set, his shrivelled complexion, and straight black lips.

The different accidents of life are not so changeable as the feelings of human nature. I had worked hard for nearly two years, for the sole purpose of infusing life into an inanimate body. For this I had deprived myself of rest and health. I had desired it with an ardour that far exceeded moderation; but now that I had finished, the beauty of the dream vanished, and breathless horror and disgust filled my heart. Unable to endure the aspect of the being I had created, I rushed out of the room and continued a long time traversing my bed-chamber, unable to compose my mind for sleep. At length lassitude succeeded to the tumult I had before endured; and I threw myself on the bed in my clothes, endeavouring to seek a few moments of forgetfulness. . . . I started from my sleep with horror; a cold dew covered my forehead, my teeth chattered, and every limb became convulsed; when, by the dim and yellow light of the moon, as it forced its way through the window-shutters, I beheld the wretch — the miserable monster whom I had created. He held up the curtain of the bed; and his eyes, if eyes they may be called, were fixed on me. His jaws opened, as he muttered some inarticulate sounds, while a grin wrinkled his cheek. He might have spoken, but I did not hear; one hand was stretched out seemingly to detain me, but I escaped, and rushed down stairs. I took refuge in the court-yard belonging to the house which I inhabited; where I remained during the rest of the night, walking up and down in the greatest agitation, listening attentively, catching and fearing each sound as if it were to announce the approach of the demoniacal corpse to whom I had so miserably given life.

from *Frankenstein; or, The Modern Prometheus* by Mary Shelley. Oxford: Oxford University Press, 1990.
Reprinted from the 1831 edition. pp. 42–43.

On the Surface

1 How would you describe the speaker?

_____

2 What has the speaker finally accomplished?

_____

3 Describe the "monster's" appearance.

_____

4 How does the speaker react to his creation?

_____

Discoveries

1 Shelley was a British writer and uses British spellings of several words. Copy three of these words; then give the American spelling of the word.

a _____

_____

b _____

_____

c _____

_____

2 Write the meanings of the following words.

a convulsive _____

b lustrous _____

c lassitude _____

d inarticulate _____

Delving More Deeply

1 Why is it ironic that the speaker is disgusted by the outcome of his work?

_____

_____

2 How does the speaker manage to sleep, knowing that the creature is in the house?

_____

3 When the creature comes to him and attempts to speak, how does the scientist respond?

_____

4 What nervous habit does the speaker engage in twice in the excerpt?

_____

Hidden Depths

1 Skim the text again, circling the many times that Shelley refers to the color yellow. What impression does the emphasis on the color yellow give?

_____

_____

_____

2 Prometheus was the god who gave fire to humans in Greek mythology; the other gods punished him harshly for this act. How is the scientist, Dr. Frankenstein, a "modern Prometheus," as the novel's subtitle calls him?

_____

_____

_____

Extend Yourself

• Find a plot summary of Shelley's novel, and explain to your classmates what happens in the story.

• Watch one of the movies based on Shelley's novel. Compare it to the plot of the novel, discussing differences with your classmates.

• Rewrite the scene from the creature's point of view. Yes, the creature is intelligent!

LESSON 28 On the Net

Cross-Curriculum Literacy Links: Technology; Arts

Text Type	Web page
Purpose	To provide information
Structure	1 Opening page
	2 Links to extra information
Features	Headlines, links, images

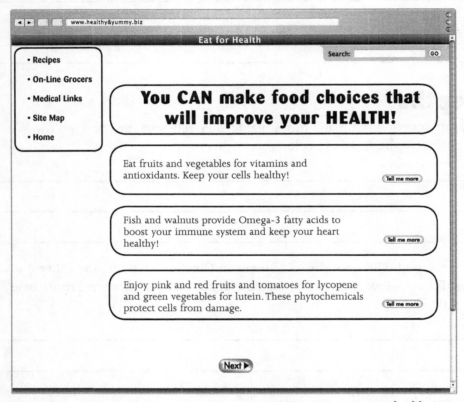

www.healthy&yummy.biz

On the Surface

1   What is the URL of this Web page? What does the .biz ending mean?

_____

2   What are the main links provided?

_____

_____

3 What products are promoted or discussed on this Web page?

_____

4 What visual elements could be used to add interest to the home page?

_____

_____

Discoveries

1 How is the content organized on this Web page? Are columns, frames, or headings used effectively? Explain.

_____

_____

_____

2 The Web page refers to vitamins, antioxidants, fatty acids, and phytochemicals. Without looking these words up, what can you guess about their meaning?

_____

_____

Delving More Deeply

1 Why does the Web page offer information as well as products?

_____

2 If you wanted to purchase organically grown blueberries, how could this Web page help you?

_____

3 Would you expect to find a recipe for double-chocolate chip cookies at the recipes link? Explain.

_____

4 Who might research healthy foods, recipes, and grocers on line?

_____

_____

Hidden Depths

1   Where do you get most of your health news: from TV, the Internet, radio, books, newspapers, or some other source? Why do you prefer your method of news gathering?

_____

_____

2   Do you consider health issues when choosing what to eat? What guides your choices?

_____

_____

_____

Extend Yourself

• Choose one of the terms — antioxidant, lutein, etc. — and find out the latest health news about it. Report your findings to your class.

• Research web sites that help people eat healthy diets. Make a list of these sites, with comments about their usefulness, to distribute to classmates.

• Construct a healthy dinner menu using the information given on the Web page in this lesson.

 **LESSON 29** **Brought to You in 3-D Terror-Vision**

Cross-Curriculum Literacy Link: Arts

Text Type	Film Festival program
Purpose	To outline two days' of films and lectures
Structure	Tabular format featuring session times and film titles
Features	Abbreviations, technical language

Marshtown Metro Theaters
is proud to announce . . .

THE BACK IN TIME SCI-FI Film Festival!

March 5 - 6

The best and the worst sci-fi movies of the 1950s!

Come in costume! Hear Professor Dougall McDonald discuss break-through film techniques of the fifties! Buy and sell sci-fi memorabilia! !

**Adults: $3.50 per film   -   Children: $2.00 per film
Two-day wrist-band pass only $25!**

	Theatre A *Sat. / Sun.*	Theatre B *Sat. / Sun.*	Theatre C *Sat. / Sun.*
12:00	*Lecture:* Black and White and Seen All Over	The Beast from 20,000 Fathoms (1953) / Robot Monster (1953)	Them! (1954) / The Thing (1951)
3:00	Forbidden Planet (1956) / The Day the Earth Stood Still (1951)	*Lecture:* Cool Electronics and Sci-Fi Soundtracks	Missile to the Moon (1959) / From Earth to the Moon (1958)
6:00	The Fly (1958) / The Return of the Fly (1959)	The Beginning of the End (1957)	*Lecture:* Out-of-this-World Special Effects
9:00	I Married a Monster from Outer Space (1958) / Plan 9 from Outer Space (1956)	The Brain from Planet Arous (1957)/ The Angry Red Planet (1959)	Queen of Outer Space (1958) / 20 Million Miles to Earth (1954)
Midnight Horror!	The Blob (1958) / It Conquered the World (1956)	Invaders from Mars (1953) / The War of the Worlds (1953)	The Attack of the Fifty-Foot Woman (1958) / The Invasion of the Body Snatchers (1956)

All movies rated G for Great!

On the Surface

1   What is the subject of the film festival?

_____

2   Are any of the movie screenings repeated?

_____

3   What is the earliest film session you can see?

_____

4   How many opportunities do you have to hear Professor McDonald lecture?

_____

5   Is this a film festival to which parents can bring their children?

_____

Discoveries

1   What is sci-fi a short expression for?

_____

2   What does the rating G stand for? Why does the ad say that it stands for "Great"?

_____

_____

Delving More Deeply

1   Read the titles of the lectures. What do they tell you about the tone and purpose of the lectures?

_____

_____

2   Is the two-day wrist-band pass a good deal for someone who wants to attend both days of the festival? Do the math and explain.

_____

_____

_____

94

3 What is memorabilia, and what kind might be on sale at the festival?

_____

_____

_____

4 Why would Marshtown Metro Theaters want to show "the worst sci-fi movies of the 1950s"?

_____

_____

Hidden Depths

1 From the film festival list, choose a movie you haven't seen. What do you think the movie is about, based on the title? Would you choose to see it? Explain.

_____

_____

_____

2 Why do you think movie theaters continue to be so popular despite the fact that films are available on video and DVD?

_____

_____

_____

Extend Yourself

- Create a poster to advertise a current sci-fi movie.

- View a movie that was made in the 1950s and then remade later (for example, *The Invasion of the Body Snatchers* or *The Fly*). Write reviews of the films and explain which version you prefer.

- One of the few color movies screening at the festival is *Forbidden Planet*. Watch this film; then research the innovative techniques used to create the soundtrack. Play part of the soundtrack for the class, explaining how it was made.

LESSON 30 A Hobbit's World

Cross-Curriculum Literacy Links: History; Geography

Text Type	Film review
Purpose	To evaluate a film
Structure	1 Context: background information
	2 Description of film (including characters and plot)
	3 Concluding statement (judgment, opinion, or recommendation)
Features	Language may be formal or informal, depending on the audience. It may include examples and quotations.

Tolkien's Towers Tops

Action/Fantasy
The Lord of the Rings: The Two Towers
(M, 180 minutes)
★★★★

Starring: Elijah Wood, Ian McKellen, Sean Astin, Bernard Hill, Liv Tyler, Viggo Mortensen, Cate Blanchett, David Wenham, Miranda Otto.

Behind the Scenes
Directed by Peter Jackson.

The plot
Must you ask? A complex tale of struggle overcoming adversity. That will have to do.
In short: Greatest show on Middle Earth.

• •

The question with any sequel — especially one as eagerly awaited as this — is whether it can match the original standard.

Mostly, sequels stink higher than a turkey three days after Christmas, but *The Two Towers* comes close to *The Fellowship of the Ring*.

That said, it is a very different movie. Where *The Fellowship* was just that, a feel-good show about a motley crew of humans, elves, hobbits and dwarves banding together for the common good, *The Two Towers* paints a much darker world, fracturing around the edges.

It also relies much less on the characters and more on superb spectacle and special effects. Move over *Ben Hur*: this film reinvents the big battle. What's more, director Peter Jackson does so without spilling a drop of blood on screen.

Jackson opens with a neat reprise of what happened when Gandalf and the hideous Balrog plunge down a cavern at the end of *The Fellowship*. It's giving nothing away to say Gandalf survives the encounter, but then the story splits in three.

The main strand concerns Frodo (Elijah Woods), Sam (Sean Astin), and the creature Gollum, who guides them on their journey to Mordor.

Amazingly, for the first time in a film, Gollum, a computer-generated image, steals the show.

In Gollum we sense one of Tolkien's central themes, the question of temptation and what a man is prepared to sacrifice to achieve power.

Gollum is the true force of darkness who wants the power bestowed by the Ring so badly he twists in agony and delivers a soliloquy Hamlet would have been proud of as good and evil war in his soul.

Which one will triumph, and is Frodo right to trust him, especially in the face of warnings from sensible Sam?

The second strand concerns the two missing Hobbits — Merry (Dominic Monaghan) and Pippin (Billy Boyd) — who are left literally out on a limb after entering the enchanted forest of Fangorn and being picked up in the branches of a walking tree called Treebeard.

The final strand belongs to the battle to save the humans, and the new players — with the exception of the spunky Miranda Otto, playing the king's niece Eowyn with a roving eye for Aragon — are not at first glance the sort you'd want in the trenches with 10,000 Urak-hai soldiers coming over the hill.

Against these heroes of the light, the battle against darkness just has to be spectacular.

It is, overwhelmingly so. There's little point in detailing the skill with which Jackson goes about his craft. It is enough to accept that better action scenes have not been filmed.

But best of all *The Two Towers* reinforces the old-fashioned message of *The Fellowship* — that through struggle against adversity, and sacrifice to a greater cause, we become better human beings.

Clark Forbes, *Sunday Herald Sun*,
29 December 2002, p. 70.

On the Surface

1 What is the difference between *The Two Towers* and the preceding film?

_____

2 How many strands are there to the story? _____

3 Why is it surprising that Gollum steals the show?

_____

4 What is the name of the enchanted forest? _____

Discoveries

1 Write the meanings of the following words.

   a soliloquy _____

   b bestowed _____

   c sequel _____

2 Why does the review use phrases such as "The main strand . . .," "The second strand . . .," and "The final strand . . ."?

_____

_____

Delving More Deeply

1 What details in this review encourage you to see the film?

_____

_____

2 Why does the reviewer not attempt to explain Jackson's techniques?

_____

_____

3 Why does the reviewer compare Gollum to Hamlet?

_____

4 What is the effect of the use of colloquial language in the review? Include some quotations to support your view.

_____

_____

_____

Hidden Depths

1 Give examples of other fantasy novels or films that are about the battle between good and evil. Why do you think fantasy literature and films are so popular at the moment?

_____

_____

_____

2 Do you rely on film reviews to make a choice about films? Would you attend a film that had been given a negative review?

_____

_____

_____

Extend Yourself

- Read Tolkien's *The Hobbit* or another fantasy novel.
- Write a 150-word soliloquy in which a character struggles between good and evil, for example, a businessman deciding whether to steal his company's profits, or a teenager contemplating shoplifting.
- Read about Jackson's filming techniques, and report your findings to the class.

LESSON 31 Selling Your Skills

Cross-Curriculum Literacy Link: Work, Employment, and Enterprise

Text Type Interview
Purpose To evaluate a candidate for a job
Structure 1 Greeting and introduction
2 Questions to elicit information
3 Responses
4 Conclusion
Features Formal language

Job Hunting

Manager: It is a pleasure to meet you, Jennifer. We were very impressed with your application to be an accountant with our firm next year. Can you tell us a few things about yourself? Perhaps your previous work experience.

Jennifer: I am a university student and in my final year of studying business. I have had a range of part-time jobs, including administrative work with an insurance firm and tutoring mathematics.

Manager: What did your administrative position involve?

Jennifer: I completed a lot of accounts payable work and bank reconciliations.

Manager: What skills did you learn there?

Jennifer: There was a lot of customer contact, so I feel that I learned to deal with people quite confidently. I had to deal with people at all levels of the organization, so this gave me an insight into the culture of the firm and how big companies work.

Manager: Did you apply any of the knowledge you are learning at the college?

Jennifer: As far as academic work, yes, a great deal was relevant. However, it was basic accounting skills that I used the most.

Manager: What do you think are your weaknesses?

Jennifer: It is hard for me to make a comment on that question. Certainly I have a lot to learn because I am only starting out, so I suppose practical knowledge is an area I am eager to build on.

Manager: What has been your worst experience at work?

Jennifer: I had an angry customer who was being unreasonable about a claim. I had to refer this matter to my supervising officer.

Manager: What are your interests outside work?

Jennifer: I love reading and going to films. I also play volleyball. I have a wide circle of friends whom I enjoy spending time with.

Manager: Do you have any questions?

Jennifer: No, not at the moment.

Manager: I have enjoyed our talk today. We have a number of applicants for this position and we will contact you with our response within two weeks.

Jennifer: Thank you for the opportunity to speak with you today.

On the Surface

1 What position is Jennifer applying for?

_____

2 What are Jennifer's qualifications?

_____

3 What jobs has she held previously?

_____

4 What are Jennifer's interests?

_____

5 What does Jennifer feel is her weakness?

_____

Discoveries

1 "Do you like cold weather?" is a closed question because the respondent will answer "yes" or "no." An open-ended question would be "Tell me how you feel about cold weather." Note that in a job interview, the questions are open. Why would this be the case?

_____

2 There are four types of sentences:

Exclamatory: I am very happy with my new car! (Expresses emotion)

Interrogative: What color is your car? (Asks a question)

Imperative: Get your car out of the way! (Gives an order)

Declarative: My car is blue. (Makes a statement)

Which sentence types would dominate in a job interview? Write an example of each sentence type.

_____

Delving More Deeply

1   Why do you think the interviewer asked about Jennifer's worst experiences at work?

   _____

   _____

2   How relevant is her academic work to the position?

   _____

3   Why does the manager not indicate whether Jennifer is or is not a successful applicant?

   _____

4   Why might the manager be interested in her skills outside work?

   _____

5   Do you think Jennifer should have asked questions at the end? Why?

   _____

Hidden Depths

1   What might Jennifer mean when she talks about the "culture" of the firm?

   _____

   _____

2   Applicants are often advised to do their homework and research a company or job thoroughly before an interview. How would you find out about a position?

   _____

   _____

Extend Yourself

- Conduct mock job interviews. Make sure you use open questions.

- Conduct a serious interview with someone who has a special responsibility in your school. Write this up and submit it for publication.

- Make up an imaginary interview with your favorite star. What questions would you ask? How do you think he or she would respond? Use ten questions.

LESSON 32 **Volunteering**

Text Type Form
Purpose To record information
Structure 1 Highly structured, logical format
              2 Specific, clear answers required
              3 Details given in categories
Features Spaces for information to be filled in

Host Family Application Form

Please write clearly.

NAME OF EXCHANGE STUDENT: _____

HOST FAMILY
Family name: _____
Father's name: _____ Age: _____
Mother's name: _____ Age: _____
Address: _____
Father's occupation: _____
Mother's occupation: _____

CHILDREN (*List names, ages, and interests of all children living at home.*)
1 _____
2 _____
3 _____
4 _____

ADDITIONAL INFORMATION
Will the student have his or her own room? _____
List the names of your children who will attend school with the exchange student. _____
_____
_____

Do you have any pets? _____

On the Surface

1 What is the purpose of the form?

_____

2 How should the form be filled in?

_____

3 What information needs to be provided by the father and mother?

_____

4 What information about the student's accommodation must be provided?

_____

Discoveries

1 Place the apostrophe in the following words.

   a the fathers job _____

   b the childrens pets _____

   c the students applications (plural subject) _____

2 Write your own rule about apostrophe use with:

   a a singular subject

   _____

   _____

   b a plural subject

   _____

   _____

3 What is the difference between it's and its?

_____

Delving More Deeply

1 Why is it important for the host-family children to attend school with the exchange student?

_____

_____

_____

2 Why is there a question about pets? What problems could pets cause?

_____

3 Why is there a question about the children's hobbies?

_____

4 Why is the age of the parents included?

_____

Hidden Depths

1 What might be the benefits of hosting an exchange student?

_____

_____

2 Write a paragraph to persuade your parents that you would like to be an exchange student.

_____

_____

_____

_____

Extend Yourself

• Design an evaluation form for exchange students at the end of their visits, for them to comment on their stay in response to your questions.

• Write a letter introducing yourself as an exchange student.

• Write a diary entry of a day in which everything went wrong in your experience as an exchange student.

 **LESSON 33** # Dear Principal

Cross-Curriculum Literacy Link: Civics and Citizenship

Text Type	Letter of Appreciation
Purpose	To express an opinion so that action will be taken
Structure	1 Name and address of company or institution
	2 Date
	3 Person to whom letter is addressed at beginning
	4 Appropriate sign off at the end
Features	Set format, formal language, loaded language

Star Students

Jim Grove, Principal
Marshtown Middle School
70 Sydney Road
Marshtown, IL 54321

08/03/07

Dear Mr. Grove,

   I am writing to thank you and your students for your invaluable help last Saturday in cleaning and preparing the gardens for our elementary school students. Without your help and the energy of your wonderful students, we would not have been able to complete the garden in time for the start of school.

   When I look at the pictures of the garden areas before Saturday, I realize how much was accomplished in just one day! Your students cleared brush and trash, weeded the beds, set out new seedlings, spread new mulch, and watered and fertilized the area. They did this work cheerfully and ably and, to my surprise, needed very little supervision, a testimony to their maturity.

   I know that many of your students have younger siblings at my school, and perhaps that is why they volunteered so willingly and effectively. I also understand, as a school principal, how much time you put into recruiting and organizing this volunteer effort.

   I hope that you and your students will stop by the gardens in a month or so to see how well everything is growing. Please share my appreciation and congratulations with your students for a job well done!

Sincerely,

Rosalyn Armache

Principal, Marshtown Elementary School

On the Surface

1 What is the reason for the letter?

_____

2 What did the writer find most impressive about the students?

_____

3 What work did the students accomplish?

_____

_____

4 What was Principal Grove's contribution to the project?

_____

Discoveries

1 Write the meanings of the following words.

a invaluable _____

b siblings _____

c recruiting _____

2 What kind of person is the writer? Justify your response by quoting examples of his use of language from the letter.

_____

_____

Delving More Deeply

1 What is the effect of the exclamation points in the letter?

_____

2 What will the garden be used for when the school year starts?

_____

_____

3 To what motive does the writer attribute the students' eagerness to help out?

_____

_____

4 What might the student volunteers have learned or gained through this experience?

_____

_____

Hidden Depths

1 Do you think it is the school's role to get students involved in volunteer work? Explain.

_____

_____

_____

2 What kinds of volunteer activities would you like to participate in? Why?

_____

_____

_____

Extend Yourself

• Lay out a garden plan for an elementary school. You may wish to look at some landscaping books to see how garden layouts are drawn. Display your layout.

• Write a formal letter of appreciation to someone who has helped you. Then send it.

• Imagine that the students had been lazy and unhelpful on the gardening day. Now write a letter of complaint from Ms. Amarche to Mr. Grove, politely yet firmly explaining the problem and demanding action to fix it.

LESSON 34 Chinese Food Tonight

Cross-Curriculum Literacy Links: Multicultural Content; Health; Mathematics

Text Type   Menu
Purpose   To inform diners of food choices
Structure   Headings, descriptions, and prices
Features   Logical groupings of dishes, descriptive phrases, prices

---

The Wok Restaurant

Sensational starters — Appetizers

Crabmeat Soup $8
*A delicate recipe from Shanghai, featuring crabmeat and
hokkien noodles in an eggwhite and chicken broth*

Coconut Chicken Soup $7
*Fragrant coconut-cream soup with succulent chicken pieces
and lemongrass*

Spicy Prawn Soup $8
Thai soup with tender prawns, mushrooms, lemongrass, and chili

Asparagus and Crabmeat Soup $7
*A sensational blend of asparagus and crabmeat, sprinkled
with zesty hot pepper*

Shanghai Spring Rolls $6
Shredded vegetables wrapped in a delicate pancake

Main Courses

Beef

Beef Szechuan $12
Szechuan-style beef tossed with red chilies and fresh orange peel

Steak Cantonese $14
*Sirloin steak lightly grilled with steamed parsnips, mushrooms,
and spinach*

Rendang Beef $15
*Aromatic Indonesian dish cooked with lemongrass, turmeric,
and tropical ginger in a spicy sauce*

Red Curry $13
*Thick red curry with tender beef, creamy coconut milk,
and crisp vegetables*

Chicken and Duck

Spicy Stir-fried Chicken $14
With broccoli and snow peas

Coconut Curry $12
*A mild curry dish that combines the delicate flavors of
chicken, carrot, coconut, and peanuts*

Mandarin Duck $12
*Shredded smoked duck, shitake mushrooms and asparagus,
served with wafer-thin pancakes*

Spicy Chicken $12
Chinese sliced chicken with hot pepper and crispy spinach

Seafood

Fish Fillet Curry $13
*A clear, fresh dish of fish fillet curry cooked
with lime and basil leaves (no coconut milk)*

Prawn Curry $12
Traditional Thai green coconut curry with prawns

King Prawns $15
*Stir-fried king prawns served with spicy dipping sauce
and fragrant steamed rice*

Deep-fried Fish $12
*Topped with a range of vegetables and smothered in
chili sauce*

Grilled Fish $13
Served with spicy seafood sauce and vegetables

Stir-fried Seafood $15
With cashew nuts in a lightly spiced sauce

Vegetarian		**Fried Rice**	$7
Stir-fried Vegetables	$10	Soft stir-fried rice with prawns, spring onions, and soy sauce	
With cashew nuts in a light sauce			
Coconut Curry	$9	Sautéed Rice Noodles	$6
With tender vegetables, tofu, and green curry paste		*With chives, bean sprouts, and Thai roasted peanuts*	
Stir-fried Noodles	$8	Thin Rice Noodles	$9
With vegetables and soybean sauce		*Stir-fried with chicken, prawns, and vegetables*	
Rice and Noodles		Fried Jasmine Rice	$6
Soft Rice Noodles	$7	*With shredded duck and minced, fresh pineapple*	
With prawns, peanuts, and tofu		Steamed Rice	$4

On the Surface

1 What kind of food appears on the appetizer menu?

_____

2 List two different countries represented on the menu.

_____

_____

3 List three different methods of cooking displayed in the menu.

_____

_____

4 Why might vegetables be described as fresh and crispy?

_____

_____

Discoveries

1 List four adjectives used in the menu to make the food sound appealing to the patrons.

_____

_____

2 What is the meaning of the following words?

a aromatic _____

b succulent _____

Delving More Deeply

1 Why do you think the word *traditional* is used in the menu to describe some dishes?

_____

_____

109

2   What is the effect of the phrase "smothered in chili sauce"?

_____

3   Why has the writer of this menu used precise lists of ingredients when describing most dishes?

_____

4   Give an example of alliteration (the repetition of consonants) in the menu, and tell why it is used.

_____

_____

Hidden Depths

1   Imagine that you have been commissioned by the manager of The Wok Restaurant to write descriptions of meals for the new Winter Special menu. Write a description of an Asian dish that you would like to see on the menu. Make sure to use descriptive language so that it sounds appealing to patrons.

_____

_____

2   Why do you think Asian food is so popular in the United States?

_____

_____

Extend Yourself

• What is the most unusual food you have ever eaten? Describe it and tell how you felt about eating it at the time.

• Create a dinner party menu for your friends, including a description of each dish.

• Create a Good Restaurant Guide for your neighborhood or city.

• Design a survey about food preferences in your age group. What do your peers like to eat? Write up a report of your findings and create a graph to display the results of your survey.

• Select a dish you are unfamiliar with and research the ingredients and method of preparation.

NAME _____   DATE _____

LESSON 35 # A Family Meal

Cross-Curriculum Literacy Links: Multicultural Content; Health

Text Type	Recipe/instructions
Purpose	Step-by-step instructions on how to do something
Structure	**1** A list of the materials required, including quantity
	2 List of equipment needed
	3 Step-by-step instructions on how to do something
	4 Length of time required
	5 Final result outlined
Features	Logical sequence of steps, may use abbreviations and technical terms

Spaghetti Bolognaise

Preparation time: 15 minutes

Total cooking time: 1 hour and 40 minutes

Serves: 4–6

Ingredients:

2 tablespoons olive oil

1 large onion, finely chopped

1 celery stick, finely chopped

2 cloves garlic, crushed

1 lb ground beef

2 cups beef stock

1 cup red wine

24 oz. can crushed tomatoes

2 tablespoons chopped fresh parsley

1 package spaghetti

parmesan cheese to serve

Method:

1 Heat the oil in a large pan. Add the onion, carrot, and celery. Cook until the onion is soft and lightly golden, stirring occasionally. Add the garlic and cook 1 more minute.

2 Add the ground beef to the pan and break it up with a fork as it cooks. When it is well browned, add the stock, wine, tomatoes, and parsley.

3 Bring to a boil; reduce the heat to very low and simmer, uncovered, for about 1½ hours, stirring occasionally. Season to taste with salt and pepper.

4 Cook the spaghetti in a large pan of boiling water until just tender (about 12 minutes). Drain well and divide among serving bowls.

5 Top the spaghetti with the bolognaise sauce, and sprinkle it with parmesan cheese. Serve immediately.

Reading Comprehension Across the Genres 8, SV1419023632

On the Surface

1 What kind of oil is used? _____

2 Does the recipe tell you exactly how long to cook the ground beef?

_____

3 What does "simmer" mean?

_____

4 How long should the spaghetti be cooked?

_____

5 What serving suggestion is made?

_____

_____

Discoveries

1 Define the following cooking terms.

a fold _____

b stir fry _____

c puree _____

2 What is the difference between "simmer" and "boil"?

_____

_____

_____

Delving More Deeply

1 What instruction is made about cooking the ground beef?

_____

_____

2 When would you start cooking the spaghetti?

_____

_____

3 List the ingredients that would need to be prepared before cooking.

_____

_____

4   What is the total cooking time?

_____

5   Why do you think it is important to serve the meal immediately?

_____

Hidden Depths

1   What foods would you buy rather than cook at home? For example, would you bake a cake or buy one?

_____

_____

2   What keeps us from cooking more? What advantages are there in being able to cook well?

_____

_____

_____

_____

Extend Yourself

•   Create an Italian food recipe book.

•   Create illustrations for the spaghetti bolognaise recipe, to make it clearer.

•   Create a poster showing different ways to serve pasta.

•   Organize a class lunch with everyone bringing an Italian dish.

Main Idea Web

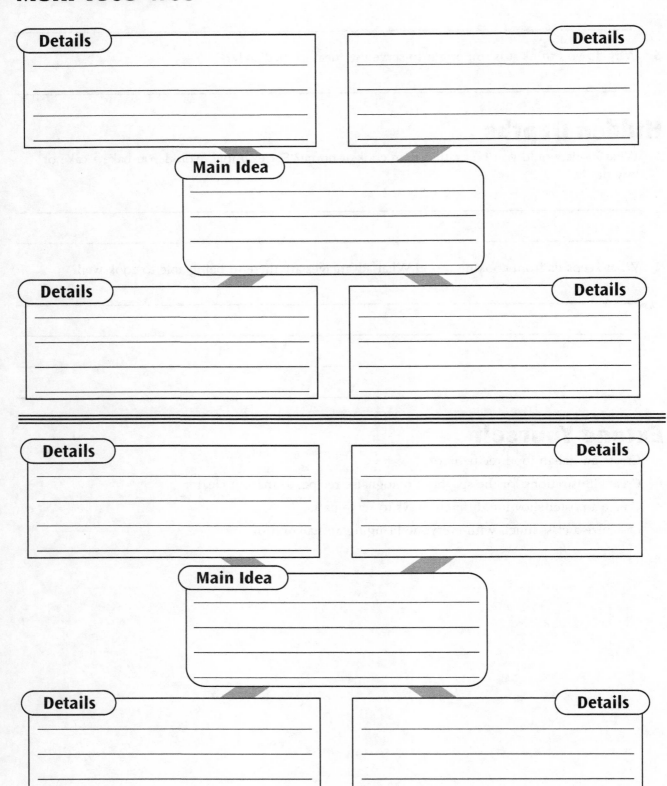

Story Map

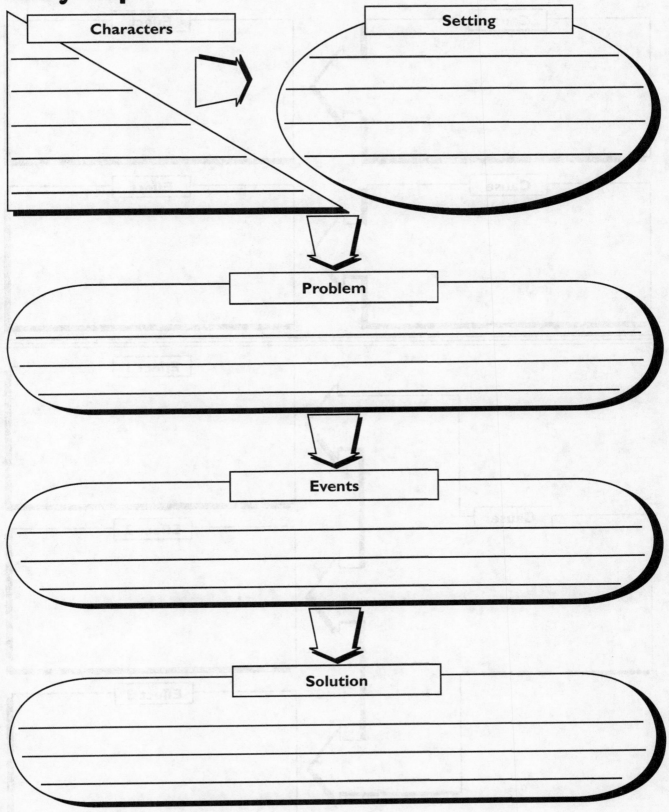

Characters

Setting

Problem

Events

Solution

Graphic Organizers: Story Map
Reading Comprehension Across the Genres 8, SV1419023632

Cause and Effect Charts

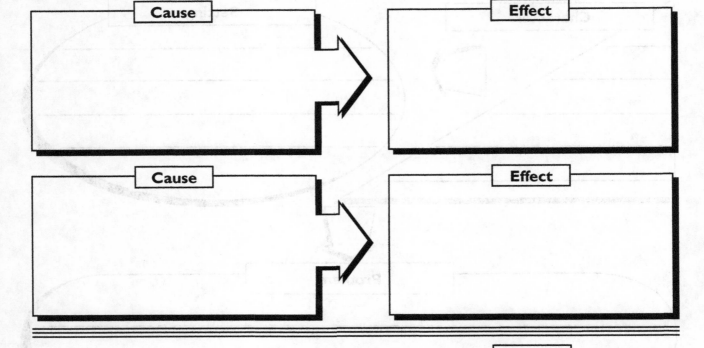

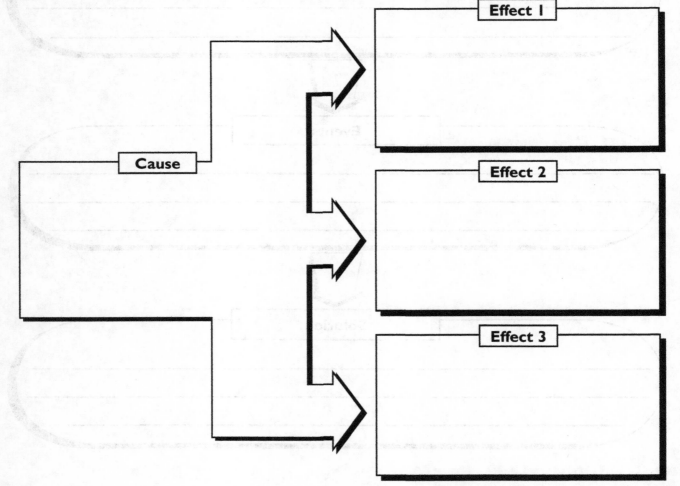

Venn Diagram

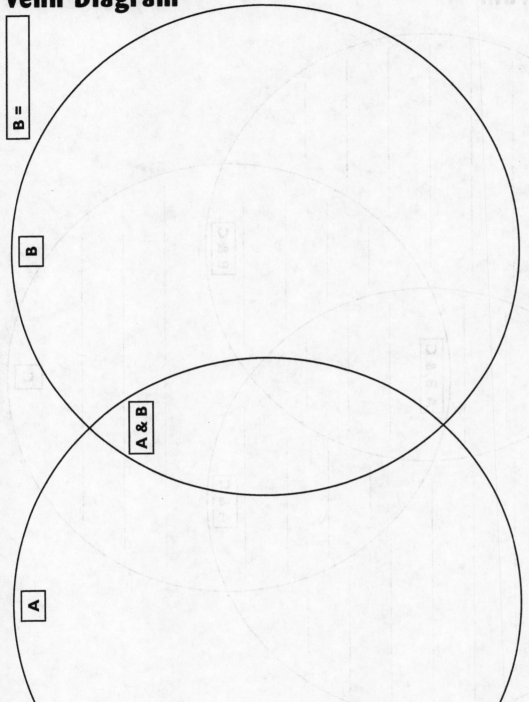

B =

B

A & B

A

A =

Venn Diagram

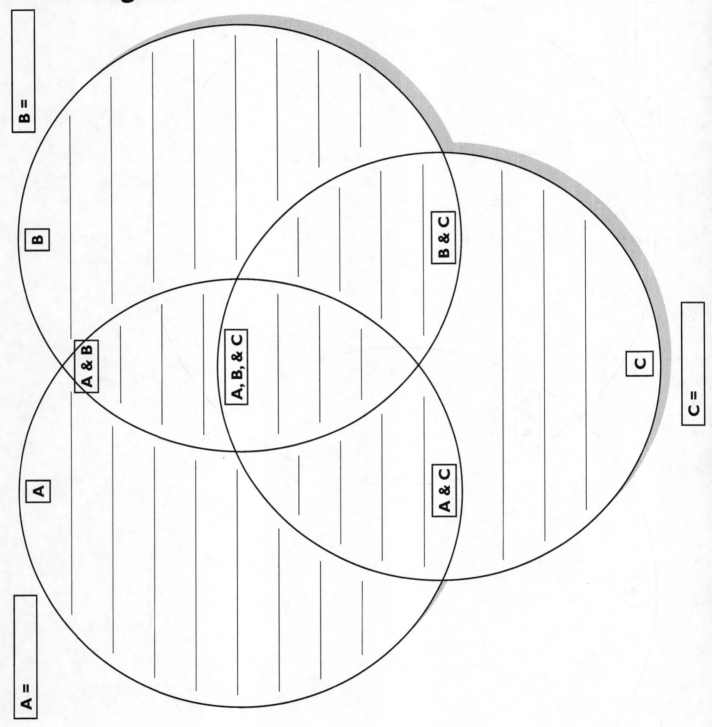

B =

B

B & C

A & B

A, B, & C

C

A

A & C

A =

C =

Word Web

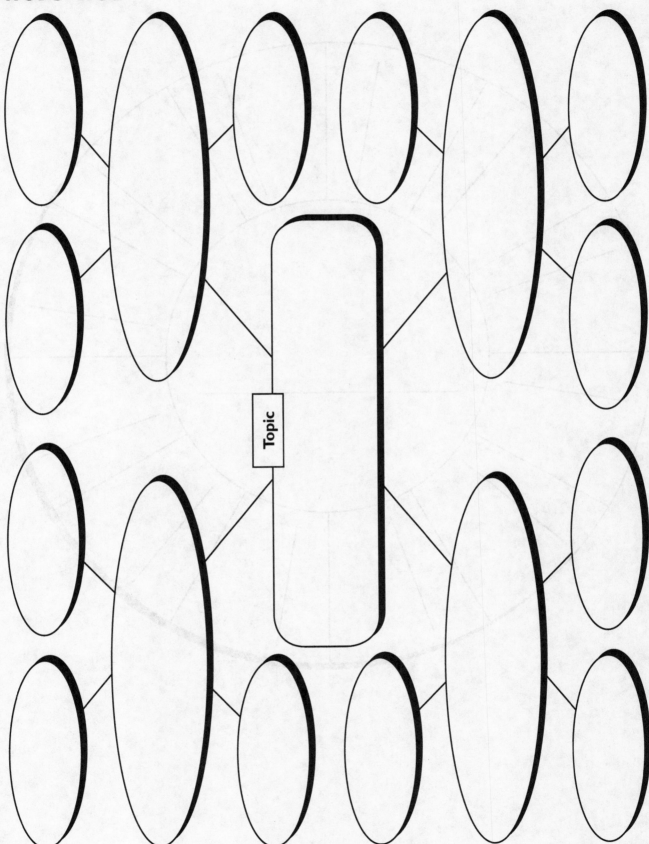

Topic

Word Wheel

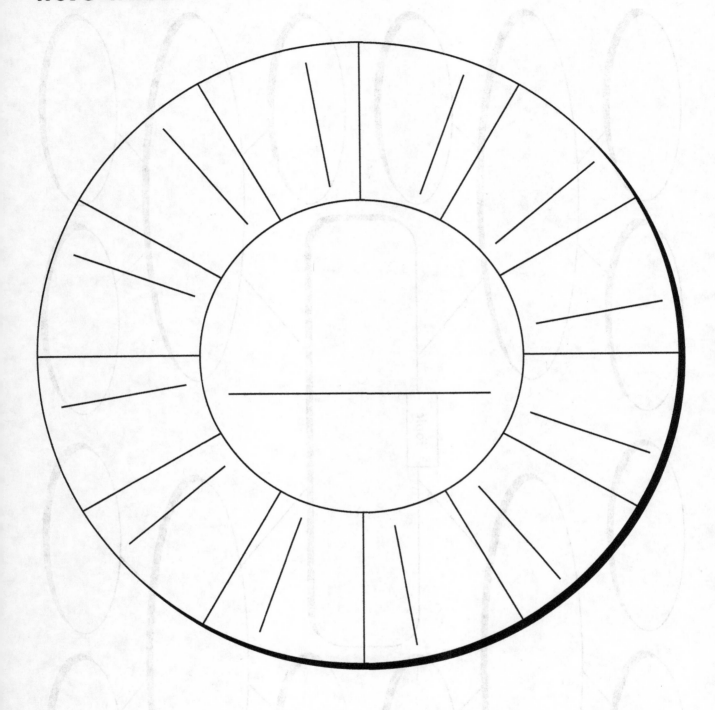

Reading Comprehension Across the Genres, Grade 8

Answer Key

Lesson 1, pages 9–11
On the Surface
1. bright, cold, windy
2. shabby, run-down
3. The lift — that is, the elevator — is not working.
4. He has a varicose ulcer and is 39 years old.
5. Thirteen o'clock; this is not our usual way of telling time.

Discoveries
1. enormous; vile; gritty; fruity
2. **a.** managed cleverly
   b. lack of substance

Delving More Deeply
1. restrained, poor living conditions, no luxuries; the description of his flat and his physical condition indicate this
2. It suggests that the population is being monitored or brainwashed or that the telescreen is there by government regulation.
3. to emphasize this fact so that no one ever forgets it
4. He dislikes the messages coming from the screen; they are an intrusion.

Hidden Depths
1. his poor physical condition and appearance; the intrusive posters and TVs; the bad condition of the building; something called Hate Week coming up
2. Responses will vary.

Lesson 2, pages 12–14
On the Surface
1. a message to the reader
2. the writer's mother
3. his sister had an accident.
4. Freekoids trashed it.
5. NukeRsol

Discoveries
1. Responses will vary.
2. a

Delving More Deeply
1. Responses will vary. Sample answer: a voice recorder
2. a nuclear holocaust; atomic jenerator, max hole in ground, gray cloud, gygered, peepil glowed, became NukeRsol, nukleea sun
3. to express the writer's feelings
4. caring and sensitive
5. Responses will vary but should be supported.

Hidden Depths
1. Responses will vary. Sample: wider use of colloquial language, new words for new technologies
2. Responses will vary. The author is young, uses colloquial language, and has little or no formal education.

Lesson 3, pages 15–17
On the Surface
1. A well-preserved, 2,300-year-old mummy has been found.
2. at the Saqarra Pyramids complex near Cairo, Egypt
3. an Egyptian-led team of Australian archeologists
4. beyond a secret door, at the bottom of a shaft
5. gold mask, turquoise beads, painted face, images of gods and goddesses and of the mummification process, bright colors

Discoveries
1. adorned, gold, beautiful, delicate, elegant
2. **a.** area containing tombs and cemeteries
   b. coffin
   c. whole, unbroken

Delving More Deeply
1. The location contains tombs and artifacts almost 2000 years older than the mummy.
2. A CT scan is like an X-ray and reveals layers of matter. The CT scan will produce images of the mummy without harming it, and will show any injuries the person had, how tall he was, etc.
3. The mask of gold, the colorful painted images, the painted face, and the delicate turquoise beadwork indicate that the person had to be wealthy and important to receive such an elegant burial.
4. A "lost" pyramid was about to be excavated.

Hidden Depths
1. They can see what the man looked like, what dieties were worshipped during his life, and what process his body underwent before burial.
2. Responses will vary. The sarcophagus's paintings stress the importance of preparing the body for proper burial.

Lesson 4, pages 18–20
On the Surface
1. fifteen
2. sales assistant in the young men's casual department
3. a written comment from a trusted person who knows you well
4. These are positive qualities for a job applicant.

Discoveries
1. a, c, d
2. The writer uses neutral words and clear sentences. He avoids slang and contractions.

Delving More Deeply
1. He seems to be conscientious and reliable.
2. A résumé is a summary of someone's work history, personal information, and qualifications. A letter of application states the applicant's interest in a job and gives some personal information that is relevant to the job.
3. English/communication skills
4. Yes, these reveal the ability to be a team player.

Hidden Depths
1. Responses will vary. Sample: Find out about the store's products and customer profile.
2. asking friends and family, searching the Internet, looking for signs in shop windows
3. Responses will vary. Sample: Teens earn money, gain skills and experience.

Lesson 5, pages 21–23
On the Surface
1. metabolism
2. metallic
3. the science that deals with the extraction and properties of metals
4. Responses will vary. Sample: burning ambition, the moon was a ghostly galleon

Discoveries
1. A simile is when two things are compared using "like" or "as"; in a metaphor, something is described as something else that it could not normally be.
2. **a.** The sun is a gold coin.
   b. The sky is a blue blanket.

Delving More Deeply
1. c
2. It shows that the word has something to do with changes.
3. Responses will vary. Sample: foan
4. This is the history of the word, especially its Greek or Latin roots.

Hidden Depths
1. Responses will vary.
2. Responses will vary.

Lesson 6, pages 24–26
On the Surface
1. Verona
2. They commit suicide. / They die.
3. an outline or opening of a play
4. The families stop fighting.
5. enemy

Discoveries
1. yes, usually
2. **a.** house; both; like; dig; y
   b. fair; ro; where; lay; scene
   c. an; grudge; to; mu; ny

Delving More Deeply
1. a
2. a
3. that it was doomed to be cut short by death
4. From ancient grudge break to new mutiny, Where civil blood makes civil hands unclean.

Hidden Depths
1. This creates a sense of dramatic irony: the audience knows the outcome, but the characters do not, and this increases the reader's or viewer's sympathy for them.
2. Responses will vary.

Lesson 7, pages 27–29
On the Surface
1. to find out the order of the chemical activity of some metals
2. They should be freshly cleaned.
3. two centimeters
4. copper, magnesium, iron, zinc
5. In the first section the metals are tested in water and in the second they are tested in acid. Also, calcium is not tested in Procedure 2.

Discoveries
1. Responses will vary.
2. Responses will vary. Sample: clean, place, record, complete

Delving More Deeply
1. chemistry
2. nine test tubes, water, the metals, acid
3. Metals vary in their reactivity to water and acid.
4. Responses will vary. Sample: It is the foundation of pharmacy.
5. Responses will vary. Sample: The procedures are simple; diagrams are probably not necessary.

Hidden Depths
1. Responses will vary.
2. Responses will vary.

Lesson 8, pages 30–32
On the Surface
1. gold, silver, copper, lead, iron, tin, mercury
2. They exist in a pure state and do not have to be separated from a compound.
3. copper
4. sodium
5. Its high chemical reactivity makes it hard to extract from compounds.

Discoveries
1. **a.** any of the known substances which consist of atoms with the same number of protons in their nuclei
   b. rocks containing metals
   c. a substance that contains two or more chemical elements
2. Sodium is the most reactive element, and it was not discovered until 1807.

Delving More Deeply
1. with electricity
2. chemistry

3. Yes, the difference between water and the chemicals. Responses will vary. Share and discuss.

Hidden Depths
1. because they are not part of a compound
2. Simple sentences are used to ensure clarity.

Lesson 9, pages 33–35
On the Surface
1. late afternoon or evening ("the sun was low in the sky")
2. frightened, scared, apprehensive: "like a crushed and frightened rabbit"; "nightmare thing"; "brain cringed"; "thankfully"; "he felt weak"; "nearly collapsed"
3. It gives him light to enter the blackness of the mine.
4. A series of questions pops into his head.
5. He is staring at himself.

Discoveries
1. **a.** to shrink in fear
   b. results of an event
   c. fragments
2. **a.** It shows that the character is timid and afraid, powerless.
   b. It shows that the sound is unexpected and therefore seems supernatural or magical.

Delving More Deeply
1. true
2. false
3. false
4. true
5. true

Hidden Depths
1. Responses will vary.
2. Responses will vary.

Lesson 10, pages 36–38
On the Surface
1. It is a campaign letter asking for voters' support.
2. Marshtown's mayor; the citizens of Marshtown
3. 10% growth in population, new businesses, new elementary schools, more traffic
4. new schools, roads, athletic complex

Discoveries
1. **a.** honor reserved for a few
   b. period of service
   c. improving
   d. park-like area of a city
2. It uses alliteration — make Marshtown marvelous — to get readers' attention and to keep the idea in their minds after they have read the letter.

Delving More Deeply
1. The writer is stressing that running a city is a job done by many people, not just the mayor.
2. a road that runs around a city's edges to ease congestion in the city center
3. Yes, the writer's tone and the subjects he discusses show that he knows how to approach his constituents and how to run a city.
4. so that the city will have a natural-looking place for people to get away from concrete and jobs and play, relax, or exercise

Hidden Depths
1. Zoning issues means deciding what kinds of homes or businesses are built in what parts of the city. They matter because people don't want a junkyard in the middle of their neighborhood or a highway near a school.
2. Responses will vary.

Lesson 11, pages 39–41
On the Surface
1. in the deep south, in the 1930s
2. He's a lawyer.
3. because he is a recluse
4. racial prejudice, growing up
5. He fights for what he believes in.

Discoveries

1. **a.** preferring one side
   b. evil
   c. focusing on the positive aspects of a situation
2. Plot is what happens; theme is the underlying idea, what the text has to say about an issue. Examples will vary.

Delving More Deeply

1. Responses will vary.
2. Responses will vary.
3. Responses will vary.
4. Responses will vary.

Hidden Depths

1. to give the reader a taste of the writer's style and to add authority to the review
2. Responses will vary.

Lesson 12, pages 42–44
On the Surface

1. Eleanor Pruitt Stewart, a woman homesteader
2. in a cabin in Wyoming, in 1909
3. A group of people dine together and then ride out a storm.
4. Responses will vary. Sample: neat, well-kept, pretty, clean

Discoveries

1. **a.** unusual
   b. preceder
   c. loud noise
2. Responses will vary.

Delving More Deeply

1. Responses will vary. Sample: to describe Gavotte, his cabin, dinner, the storm
2. floor was so white; windows shone; square home-made table, every inch scrubbed; pounded until it was clean and sweet
3. He is an able man, proud of his home and gracious to guests.
4. to give readers a sense of how it sounded and to personify it as something almost alive and threatening

Hidden Depths

1. They put her in an imaginative, dreamy state. Responses will vary.
2. The wildness of the storm inspires the wildness in his playing.

Lesson 13, pages 45–47
On the Surface

1. a tree being cut down
2. one hundred years
3. saddened
4. to be overpowered by wind or storm
5. "She leaned forward," "sad abruptness," "limpness of foliage," "folding of limbs," "graceful beauty," "better for her," "forest giant," "left her"

Discoveries

1. **a.** soft, low talking that is unclear
   b. suddenness
   c. certainty
2. Responses will vary.

Delving More Deeply

1. It makes us see the incident as something tragic.
2. sad abruptness, limpness of foliage, final folding, leaves pale blended with the morning rain, ignoble inevitability, pain, saddened, loss
3. that trees are noble and we should realize their significance in nature and in our lives
4. that although he is experiencing a loss, he is also experiencing a gain because the wood and lumber from the tree will be used

Hidden Depths

1. Responses will vary.
2. Responses will vary.

Lesson 14, pages 48–50
On the Surface

1. the printing press
2. They were very complicated and expensive to make.

---

3. in big Italian towns
4. how to count to 12
5. 15 minutes a day

Discoveries

1. **a.** predicted
   b. something new
   c. contrary to Church teachings
2. Responses will vary.

Delving More Deeply

1. The clock marked the ending of human history when time was told by observing the heavenly bodies and the beginning of human history when time was told by mechanical devices.
2. It was a center for everything: meeting, information, etc.
3. in the mid 1600s
4. to spread knowledge, to increase the number of people who could read

Hidden Depths

1. Responses will vary.
2. Responses will vary.

Lesson 15, pages 51–53
On the Surface

1. Brazil
2. Ecuador and Brazil
3. Buenos Aires
4. North Atlantic, South Atlantic, and the Pacific Ocean

Discoveries

1. a square
2. Symbols will vary.

Delving More Deeply

1. UK, the United Kingdom
2. Bolivia
3. North America
4. Countries on the equator — Ecuador and Brazil — would probably be warmest because they are farther from the two poles and never have a season when the sun is farther away from them.

Hidden Depths

1. There was a war there in the 1980s.
2. Spanish

Lesson 16, pages 54–56
On the Surface

1. a bar graph
2. 237 votes
3. 35%
4. 18%
5. 119

Discoveries

1. They did not have a strong preference about the field trip.
2. for clear communication and because of the lack of space

Delving More Deeply

1. Probably — this number represents a likely number of eighth graders at a school.
2. so that students have a say in the activities planned for them
3. to the water park

Hidden Depths

1. They can take another poll that lists only these two options.
2. Responses will vary. Polls are supposed to track public opinion about an issue so that lawmakers and others in authority can represent the people who elected them.

Lesson 17, pages 57–59
On the Surface

1. a possum; trichosaurus cunninghamii
2. It was thought to be the same as possums in other parts of Australia.
3. Dr. David Lindenmayer
4. through genetic testing

Reading Comprehension Across the Genres 8, SV1419023632

Discoveries
1. **a.** afflicted
   b. people who guard or look after something
   c. varied
2. **a.** end-of-year
   b. bell-shaped

Delving More Deeply
1. The Victorian possums have larger ears, longer feet, shorter tails, and a flatter face.
2. that we must take care to identify species before they are wiped out; responses will vary
3. wet forest areas
4. the study of the environment

Hidden Depths
1. Reponses will vary.
2. Reponses will vary.

Lesson 18, pages 60–62
On the Surface
1. nineteenth-century factories
2. A woman named Deborah is taking supper to a man working in an iron mill.
3. Hugh
4. the cold, the rain, the darkness, the distance, her tiredness, and her aching back

Discoveries
1. **a.** sneaking, creeping
   b. guards on watch
   c. criticism
   d. dense, slow in thought
2. Since Deb is taking food to someone at the mill, they are probably poor, and the time period indicated by their speech also likely means that if they're poor, they're uneducated.

Delving More Deeply
1. cold, dark rain contrasted with hot, bright fire
2. All that matters to the mill owners is their ability to do work with their hands. They are not fully human, at least while they are at work.
3. that it is a hellish place and pitiless to those who live and work in it
4. She is so very tired that she can sleep on a pile of iron bits with the fires blazing around her and the deafening noise of the machines in her ears.

Hidden Depths
1. Responses will vary.
2. They are in danger of being burned, hurting muscles, being cut. The narrator pities and sympathizes with them.

Lesson 19, pages 63–65
On the Surface
1. sweet gelatin
2. people who like gelatin; people who want to make an easy dessert; people who don't like to cook
3. It's easy to make and tastes good.
4. Mac, swell; buck up; little woman; cinch

Discoveries
1. Now is; it is; we will; they will
2. Little trouble: a bit of trouble; Little woman: a term used, sometimes negatively, in the mid-twentieth century to mean "the wife"

Delving More Deeply
1. 1950s
2. the visuals; the wording; the sexual stereotyping; the man's hairstyle and apron; the old fashioned mixer
3. that they cannot cook; that their wives would be surprised and pleased if they did anything domestic
4. that they are good cooks and housekeepers; that they are inferior in general to their husbands; that men are their inferiors in the kitchen

Hidden Depths
1. Responses will vary.
2. Responses will vary.

Lesson 20, pages 66–68
On the Surface
1. that cell phones are expensive and overused
2. to allow parents to contact their children; for business
3. They are costly, unsociable, annoying, and may emit too much radiation.
4. It lets readers know that the article is likely to be negative about cell phones.
5. that people save money by having land line phones and that cell phones emit dangerous radiation

Discoveries
1. **a.** about to happen
   b. devilish
   c. send out, give off
   d. madness, obsession
2. Responses will vary.

Delving More Deeply
1. craze, ridiculous, corny, diabolical, mania
2. Responses will vary. Sample: Do you really need to IM your friend at all hours of the day?
3. chatting on the phone loudly in public places, such as on public transport and in restaurants
4. Responses will vary. Sample: businesspeople; real estate agents; doctors

Hidden Depths
1. Responses will vary.
2. Responses will vary.

Lesson 21, pages 69–71
On the Surface
1. to explain how to use a MicroPro Deluxe microwave
2. Using the Timer, Using the MicroTime Feature, Important Safety Precautions, Service; they are in bold type and set to the left
3. 1-800-555-OVEN
4. 10
5. under Important Safety Precautions

Discoveries
1. **a.** watch; Sentences will vary.
   b. ended, is over; Sentences will vary.
   c. service person; Sentences will vary.
2. Timer, Start, MicroTime, Power Level (also numbers 1–10); the function buttons each start with a capital letter

Delving More Deeply
1. Yes; it rotates the food for more even cooking
2. **a.** They may explode.
   b. It could boil over and burn your hands.
3. The regular timer does not shut off the oven; MicroTime does

Hidden Depths
1. Responses will vary.
2. Responses will vary.

Lesson 22, pages 72–74
On the Surface
1. because we collect them on every shopping expedition
2. 25 cents per bag
3. billions
4. a 90 per cent reduction in bag usage
5. loss of jobs in the plastics industry, less convenience for shoppers

Discoveries
1. **a.** cost
   b. uncommon thing
   c. supervising, managing

2. Responses will vary. Sample: in order to keep people on the writer's side; to make a suggestion rather than alienate people with a demand
3. a, c

Delving More Deeply
1. to give the piece more credibility
2. This is inclusive language and involves the reader in the issue.
3. It provides a visual reminder of the damage caused by plastic bags.
4. Responses will vary. Sample: to counteract the possible arguments against the idea
5. more experts and loaded language, more examples, more statistics, more imagery, more information about the consequences of pollution

Hidden Depths
1. Responses will vary.
2. Responses will vary.

Lesson 23, pages 75–77
On the Surface
1. on a school playground during recess
2. their teacher
3. Some look anxious, others interested or entertained.
4. It is some sort of totem that gives him the "floor" to speak while everyone listens.

Discoveries
1. Satire is designed to make us laugh but also to teach us a lesson. Satire uses sarcasm to ridicule a person or thing.
2. Satire uses laughter as a weapon and as a lesson, not just to make people laugh or entertain them.

Delving More Deeply
1. people who watch so much TV that they start to confuse TV with life
2. You need to know that the speaker is referring to a show in which contestants for a large cash prize get "voted off the island" until only one is left.
3. It is funny because he is treating the class as if it is a competitive TV show. It is inappropriate because he should be teaching them or supervising their play.
4. Responses will vary. The teacher is being ridiculed, because he refers to the TV show in his speech. Perhaps the children, who are watching him with fascination, are also being ridiculed.

Hidden Depths
1. Responses will vary.
2. Responses will vary.

Lesson 24, pages 78–80
On the Surface
1. They are looking for more time to spend preparing for standardized tests.
2. They are not wise and do not increase academic success.
3. that music does indeed matter and that schools are making mistakes
4. math

Discoveries
1. a. endurance
   b. a requirement, a necessity
   c. classmates
2. PE — physical education; SAT — Scholastic Aptitude Test; MRI — magnetic resource imaging

Delving More Deeply
1. false
2. false
3. false
4. a. true
   b. false
   c. true
   d. true

Hidden Depths
1. Responses will vary.
2. Responses will vary.

Lesson 25, pages 81–83
On the Surface
1. Her dog was protective of her during an illness.
2. They show concern in their eyes and by staying close by the sick person.
3. when they are allowed to sniff the body of the deceased
4. by observing a change in body language or detecting an odor
5. The lively dog became calm.

Discoveries
1. weak, needing protection
2. understand deeply
3. given off
4. using a thought process

Delving More Deeply
1. scent hormones
2. Responses will vary. Sample: told in a personal way, first-person voice, paragraphs are longer, many anecdotes
3. to give the article credibility
4. all, but especially owners of dogs or cats

Hidden Depths
1. Responses will vary. Share and discuss.
2. Responses will vary. Share and discuss.

Lesson 26, pages 84–86
On the Surface
1. one hour
2. four
3. 6:00 A.M.–10:00 P.M.
4. most frequent: Step; least frequent: Sculpt
5. 12 instructors: Jo, Chris, David, Jenny, Karen, Kevin, Bill, Jim, Phil, Lyn, Janice, Gerry

Discoveries
1. a. stamina
   b. stress, focus
   c. effort, work
2. Responses will vary.

Delving More Deeply
1. Most people work or are in school in the afternoons.
2. personal trainers, treadmills, weight training room, sauna, whirlpool, café, etc.
3. to rehydrate during exercise
4. to warn people that they need to be able to follow complicated instructions and perform dance steps

Hidden Depths
1. improved general health, heart fitness, weight control, strength, muscular development, increased energy and well-being
2. Responses will vary.

Lesson 27, pages 87–89
On the Surface
1. a scientist driven to achieve something grand
2. He has brought a corpse to life.
3. He is unnaturally hideous; his features do not go together; his eyes are dull.
4. He flees in disgust and fear.

Discoveries
1. a. burnt — burned
      endeavoured — endeavored
   b. endeavouring — endeavoring
   c. ardour — ardor
2. a. jerky, uncoordinated
   b. shiny, lush
   c. exhaustion
   d. unclear

Delving More Deeply

1. He had poured every bit of time and energy into the work for almost two years.
2. Exhaustion overcomes him.
3. He flees in terror before trying to understand the creature.
4. He paces back and forth, first in his bedroom and then in the courtyard.

Hidden Depths

1. Responses will vary. Sample: The yellow moonlight, candle-light, eye color, and skin give the text a sickly feel. Nothing is clean or pure or bright — all the light is only almost light.
2. Prometheus gave humans something the gods thought they shouldn't have. They weren't ready for fire and all its power. Dr. Frankenstein, too, is trying to steal a godly power — the power to give life.

Lesson 28, pages 90–92
On the Surface

1. healthy&yummy.biz; it is a business Web page that sells products or services
2. recipes, on-line grocers, medical links, site map, home, and links to more information on the health statements
3. fruits and vegetables, fish and nuts
4. Responses will vary. Share and discuss.

Discoveries

1. Responses will vary.
2. that they name nutrients that healthy foods provide to keep the body healthy and strong

Delving More Deeply

1. The information is free and draws viewers in; then they may buy products.
2. It provides links to on-line grocers, where you can order the berries.
3. No, this is a Web page that promotes making healthy food choices.
4. Responses will vary. Sample: students, researchers, those who prefer shopping on-line or who live far from large grocery stores

Hidden Depths

1. Responses will vary.
2. Responses will vary.

Lesson 29, pages 93–95
On the Surface

1. science fiction movies made in the 1950s
2. *The Beginning of the End* is shown on Saturday and Sunday at 6:00 P.M.
3. 12:00 noon
4. three each day of the festival
5. Yes, the movies were made in the 1950s and have G ratings.

Discoveries

1. science fiction
2. It stands for General Audiences, but the ad is playing with the rating to make a point that the movies are fun to watch.

Delving More Deeply

1. The titles make the lectures sound fun and entertaining, not scholarly and formal.
2. Yes. To see ten movies, which would be possible in two days, would cost $35 for an adult, so the wrist band saves $10. For a child, 10 movies would cost $20, so the wrist band would not be a savings.
3. Memorabilia is collectible items having to do with something from the past. The memorabilia at the festival will probably be movie posters, t-shirts, action figures, outer space stuff.
4. Responses will vary. Sample: Sci-fi film buffs find old, bad sci-fi movies funny and entertaining.

Hidden Depths

1. Responses will vary.
2. Responses will vary. Sample: It's fun to go to the movies with friends; the big screen and the sound improve the entertain-ment; some special effects are better on the big screen; it's nice to get out of the house.

Lesson 30, pages 96–98
On the Surface

1. *The Two Towers* is much darker, relies more on spectacle and special effects.
2. three
3. He is a computer-generated character.
4. Fangorn

Discoveries

1. **a.** monologue in which the character speaks to himself
   b. given
   c. following part
2. This structures the review and helps readers make sense of a complex plot.

Delving More Deeply

1. It is as good as the original and has impressive special effects and battle scenes.
2. He cannot do justice to Jackson's abilities and asks readers to trust his assessment that "better action scenes have not been filmed."
3. Both deliver stirring soliloquies.
4. Responses will vary.

Hidden Depths

1. Responses will vary. Share and discuss.
2. Responses will vary. Share and discuss.

Lesson 31, pages 99–101
On the Surface

1. accountant
2. She is in her final year of a business degree.
3. part-time work tutoring math and administrative work with an insurance firm
4. reading, films, volleyball, being with friends
5. lack of practical knowledge

Discoveries

1. Open-ended questions elicit more information.
2. interrogative and declarative; examples will vary

Delving More Deeply

1. Responses will vary. Sample: to see if she is honest and to see how she would handle a crisis
2. very relevant, since accounting is an important part of the business world
3. because there are other applicants
4. because these indicate that she is a well-rounded person, someone with personality and a social life
5. Yes, questions show interest in the position and knowledge about the business.

Hidden Depths

1. the way things are done in a certain place; the way people are addressed, the expectations of staff, etc.
2. by looking up the company on the Internet, asking questions, picking up promotional material

Lesson 32, pages 102–104
On the Surface

1. to allow a family to apply to host an exchange student
2. clearly, either written or typed
3. name, occupation, age
4. whether the student will have his or her own room

Discoveries

1. **a.** father's
   b. children's
   c. students'
2. **a.** The apostrophe always goes before the *s* is added, as in "the *boy's* guitar." A proper noun ending in -*s* may use *'s* or just *'*, as in *James's* (or *James'*) book.
   b. The apostrophe goes after the final *s*, as in *ladies'*. For some irregular plurals, it goes before the final *s*, as in *men's*.
3. *It's* is a contraction of "it is"; *its* represents ownership or possession.

Delving More Deeply

1. Responses will vary. Sample: so the exchange student is comfortable and will know someone in the new school; so that he or she can be oriented to the host country's culture
2. Some people do not like animals in the house or may be allergic to them.
3. This will be of interest to the exchange student.
4. so the student receives a clear picture of the family

Hidden Depths

1. Responses will vary.
2. Responses will vary.

Lesson 33, pages 105–107

On the Surface

1. to express appreciation for student volunteers and the work they did
2. They were mature enough not to need much supervision.
3. They cleared brush and trash, weeded beds, set out new seedlings, spread new mulch, and watered and fertilized the area.
4. He recruited students and organized the work day.

Discoveries

1. **a.** priceless
   b. brothers and sisters
   c. asking people to sign up for a job
2. Responses will vary. Sample: someone who values hard work and helpful ways; "They did this work cheerfully and ably . . . ."

Delving More Deeply

1. They emphasize the writer's sense of gratitude.
2. Responses will vary. Sample: Students will eat lunch there, play there, learn how things grow, tend the plants, eat food that grows.
3. She thinks they had their younger siblings who would use the garden in mind.
4. Responses will vary. Sample: a good feeling for having helped; knowledge and skills for future gardening; a fun day outside with friends; brisk exercise

Hidden Depths

1. Responses will vary.
2. Responses will vary.

Lesson 34, pages 108–110

On the Surface

1. soups and one finger-food item, spring rolls
2. Indonesia, Thailand, China
3. stir fry, sauté, grill, steam
4. to emphasize the high quality and healthiness of the ingredients

Discoveries

1. sensational, delicate, fragrant, succulent, tender, zesty, aromatic, spicy, tender, crisp, mild, crispy, clear, fresh, light
2. **a.** fragrant
   b. tender, juicy

Delving More Deeply

1. to emphasize that the dish is an authentic standard of the culture's cuisine
2. Responses will vary. Sample: to suggest abundance
3. so readers gain a clear understanding of the flavors before they order
4. creamy coconut; to add flair to the descriptions and entice readers to order the item

Hidden Depths

1. Responses will vary.
2. Responses will vary.

Lesson 35, pages 111–113

On the Surface

1. olive
2. no, just cook till well browned
3. to cook at a temperature at or just below boiling
4. about 12 minutes
5. Sprinkle with parmesan cheese.

Discoveries

1. **a.** to mix one ingredient into another very gently
   b. to fry quickly over high heat while stirring
   c. to whip in a blender or food processor till smooth and creamy
2. boil: to cook liquid or food in liquid at that is boiling; simmer: to cook food in water that is at or just below boiling point

Delving More Deeply

1. Break it up with a fork and cook until it is well browned.
2. when the bolognaise sauce was nearly ready
3. onion, carrot, celery, garlic, parsley
4. one hour and 40 minutes
5. because the dish needs to be hot and spaghetti will go limp

Hidden Depths

1. Responses will vary.
2. Responses will vary.

Acknowledgments

The authors and publisher gratefully credit or acknowledge permission to reproduce extracts from the following sources.

The Advertising Archive Ltd., advertisement "Now's the time for Jell-O"; Children's Leisure Products Ltd., extract from *Traveler's Atlas of the World*, Geddes & Grosset, Scotland, 2000; Clark Forbes, extract from Clark Forbes, "Tolkien's towers tops" in *Sunday Herald Sun*, Melbourne, 29/12/2002; Macmillan Education, extracts from Jack Davis, "Death of a tree," in John and Dorothy Colmer (eds), *Through Australian Eyes: Prose and Poetry for Schools*, Macmillan, South Melbourne, 1984; Pan Macmillan, extract from Ray Bradbury, "The Meteor" in Peter Haining (ed.) *Classic Science Fiction*, Pan, London, 1998; Mary Papadakis, extract from Mary Papadakis, "Hello my possum" in *Sunday Herald Sun*, Melbourne, 12/1/2003; Penguin Books Australia Ltd, extract from Geoffrey Blainey, *A Short History of the World*, Penguin Books Australia, Camberwell, 2000; *Pets n People Magazine*, extract from Lyndal Kelley, 'How do pets know when we are sick or sad?' in *Pets n People*, vol. 4, issue 23, 2002; Scholastic Australia, extract from "A messij 2 the reeda" in CBD by John Heffernan. Text copyright © John Heffernan, 2000. First published by Margaret Hamilton Books, a division of Scholastic Australia Pty Limited, 2000. Reproduced by permission of Scholastic Australia Pty Limited.

Every attempt has been made to trace and acknowledge copyright holders. Where the attempt has been unsuccessful, the publisher welcomes information that would redress the situation.